The Indian Origins of Modern Economic Growth

Modern economic growth first emerged in Britain and then spread to a few other countries in western Europe and the USA. This book argues that it is her control over India which put Britain at the apex of the world economy in the nineteenth century, and it is British policies and actions, based on her Indian foundation, which led to the globalisation of the nineteenth century – a globalisation very different from the previous globalisations in history.

Technological innovations of the nineteenth century were embedded in that globalisation process. It is this which ensured that growth and innovations would not peter out this time, as they had after various "efflorescences" in history. While the increased availability of silver from the Mexican and Peruvian mines in the sixteenth and seventeenth centuries, and the Atlantic slave trade both had important consequences for global development, the decisive disjuncture that opened the path to modern economic growth was the British victory in the Battle of Plassey (1757), which in due course led to the colonisation of the whole of the subcontinent.

The book is likely to be of interest to a diverse readership, beyond those interested in economic history and growth economics.

Prabir Bhattacharya is an economist affiliated to both Glasgow and Heriot-Watt Universities. He is editor-in-chief of the *Journal of Interdisciplinary Economics* and was formerly editor-in-chief of the *Progress in Development Studies*. He has taught at various universities including the University College London, University of Edinburgh, Yokohama National University, Kobe University and the University of Science and Technology, Beijing.

The Indian Origins of Modern Economic Growth

Colonialism and the Rise of Britain and Europe

Prabir Bhattacharya

Routledge
Taylor & Francis Group
LONDON AND NEW YORK

First published 2026
by Routledge
4 Park Square, Milton Park, Abingdon, Oxon OX14 4RN

and by Routledge
605 Third Avenue, New York, NY 10158

Routledge is an imprint of the Taylor & Francis Group, an informa business

British Library Cataloguing-in-Publication Data
A catalogue record for this book is available from the British Library

ISBN: 978-1-041-20163-2 (hbk)
ISBN: 978-1-041-20164-9 (pbk)
ISBN: 978-1-003-71536-8 (ebk)

DOI: 10.4324/9781003715368

Typeset in Times New Roman
by Newgen Publishing UK

To Pratik, Shreya, Chitra, and Sanghamitra

Contents

Acknowledgements

This is my "Japan book". The seed of this book was planted in the library of Yokohama National University (YNU) in 2001. I was visiting the University as a guest professor in the Faculty of Economics. One morning, early in my stay, I went to the university library to browse. It was well stocked, with an excellent collection of journals, but only a handful of books in English, probably numbering no more than 500. These books were on various subjects – from natural sciences to social sciences to humanities – all shelved together in one corner of the library. While browsing, I picked up, serendipitously (as it turned out), a book on Irish history – and as it happened the only book on history on that shelf. As I flipped through its pages, I found that the author (whose name and title of the book now escapes me) was talking about Ireland having been a periphery of England. This rang a bell. I was familiar with the core-periphery models in development economics and in new economic geography then in vogue. I had also, not too long before, moved from England to Scotland and had become aware of the divide between the east and west coasts of Scotland. I decided at that moment in the library that I needed to learn about the Irish and Scottish history.

My knowledge of history was rudimentary, little beyond what I had been taught in my high school in India. My knowledge of economic history was non-existent. As I read on Scottish, Irish and then global history, I become aware of the role that the British control of India played in the evolution of the world economy in the nineteenth century. I thought that someday I might want to write an article on this, but other preoccupations were more pressing.

Meanwhile, I had continued to visit Japan intermittently to give occasional lectures and to participate in conferences. Then in 2017 I was invited back for a longer stay, first at the Research Institute for Economics and Business Administration (RIEB) at Kobe University, and then at YNU. At both universities, I was given plenty of time and facilities to do my research. While at Kobe, I gave a seminar on the topic of "The rise of Europe". I received some very constructive feedback and decided to put pen to paper. The draft of that article, subsequently published in the *Journal of Interdisciplinary Economics* (and which now constitutes, with minor changes, the Chapter 2 of this monograph) was written at YNU. I thank both Kobe and YNU for inviting me and making this research possible. I made many good friends in Japan over the years, and I would particularly like to thank Yasushi Nakamura, Takahiro Sato, Manabu Furuta, Koji Takahashi, and Royojon Mitomo for many a good discussion and the good times that I had with them.

The prompt for writing this book came from Andy Humphries at Routledge. Andy had approached me, having read my article in the *JIE*, to enquire whether I would be interested in expanding the ideas in that article into a monograph. Once I had said yes, he gently and at regular intervals kept encouraging me to complete it. He also provided feedback on an outline plan. I am truly grateful.

My friends Thomas Torrance, Annie Miller and Paul Hare have read parts of the manuscript and made constructive suggestions. As ever, I am indebted to them.

As the readers will see, in many places, I have drawn heavily on the works of others. This book would not have been possible without their prior work. I acknowledge my debt to them.

My debt to my wife, Chitra, and our twins, Shreya and Pratik, has grown over time. Chitra has been unwavering in her support all through and the twins, now on the cusp of young adulthood, have continued to help in a myriad of ways. My long-distance conversations with my sister, Sanghamitra, have also proved most helpful. I thank and dedicate this book to all four of them.

1 Introduction

Modern economic growth first emerged in Britain. Growth then spread to a few other countries in Western Europe and the USA. Goldstone (2015) has defined modern economic growth as being one that is characterised by both significant population growth and significant per capita income growth on a long-term sustainable basis. This seems as good a working definition as any, particularly in the context of the discussions proposed in this book. There have been recent reconstructions of historical GDP data for a number of countries by a number of scholars.[1] A close examination of these data shows that "at no point after 1600 and before 1780 did any nation in Europe experience both significant population growth and significant per capita income growth, as would be necessary for modern economic growth to have emerged" (Goldstone 2015, p. 1). The data further show that, for Britain, almost all of its per capita growth between 1270 and 1780 came in two concentrated bursts: one in the late 1300s (1350–1400) after the Black Death, and the other in the late 1600s (1650–1700) when population again declined (due to increased mortality, caused, among others, by outbreaks of the plague, chronic diseases and poor weather). GDP growth sharply declined after the 1690s when population growth resumed and seems to fade away almost entirely before the 1780s. And according to estimates by Crafts (1985) and Crafts and Harley (1992), significant per capita income growth is discernible in Britain only from the 1830s or so. Similarly, the Dutch GDP per capita in 1800–1807 were only 5 per cent above previous peaks in the 1590s and 1640s. And "after the 1640s, all the way up to the 1800s, the only gains that occur in GDP/capita were entirely the result of a decline in Holland's population".

DOI: 10.4324/9781003715368-1

History offers examples of several episodes of rapid growth, separated by centuries of stagnation. Goldstone (2002) has called these episodes "efflorescences". An efflorescence is "a relatively sharp, often unexpected upturn in significant demographic and economic indices", which then peters out. Examples include the Golden Age of Islam, the Song dynasty in China, the height of the Qing dynasty in China and the Renaissance Italy.[2] They were all associated with an expansion of trade. None of these episodes, however, resulted in a sustained and significant growth in per capita income. As we know, they all petered out (for various reasons). But the process which started in the late eighteenth-century Britain has lasted. Why? In answering this question, it is important to begin by recognising – and as Malanima (2021) has pointed out after a careful analysis of the data – that there was nothing in the prior growth patterns that made Britain, or Europe, uniquely likely to achieve the breakthrough to modern economic growth. Or, as Goldstone (2021) has put it, "… the emergence of modern economic growth after 1750 has to be understood as something that emerged rather late and suddenly, and was not prefigured, much less caused, by a distinctive pre-industrial pattern of growth in GDP/cap".

We shall argue that the most important reasons behind the emergence of modern economic growth are to be found in the British control of India and Indian resources from 1757 onwards; that it was her control of India that put Britain at the apex of the world economy. And it is British policies and actions, based on her Indian foundation, which led to the establishment of a globalised world economy of a kind very different from the previous "globalisations" that had occurred in history (be it the "globalisation" under Rome, along the Silk Roads, or "globalisation" of the sixteenth century).[3] It is this globalisation and the forces leading towards this globalisation which made all the difference.

This new globalisation as it developed had, among its various features, the following ones which we believe to have been particularly significant, viz., (i) the establishment of British ascendancy and then British supremacy in the global economy; (ii) the huge amount of foreign investment undertaken by leading economies, mostly by Britain and mostly in infrastructure development; (ii) increasingly, the export of manufactured goods produced by the "core" for primary products produced by the "periphery"; (iii) the huge volume of overseas emigration (both forced and otherwise); (iv) the use of sterling as an international currency; (v) the development of a well-functioning multilateral payment mechanism that came to encompass most parts of the world and (vi) last but not the least, the gradual establishment of an overarching global financial system based on the City of London (the financial hub of London). And all of the above was underpinned by a generally peaceful nature of the world for the major European powers between 1815 and 1913. The apogee of this globalisation was reached in the years between 1870 and 1914.

It is the globalising forces, set in motion and propelled by British policies and actions, based on her Indian foundation, which ensured that growth would not peter out this time and that the progress in technology would continue. Technological innovations of the nineteenth century, we shall argue, were embedded in the nineteenth-century globalisation process. However, it is the case that the forces which led to the transformation of Western Europe and European offshoots (via globalisation) also contributed to the falling behind of India and China (India under the British rule and China under a weak state and Western predations). The great transformation and the great divergence were closely linked. The great transformation was also associated with the convergence in incomes within the Atlantic economy, with many of the poorer countries in the European periphery growing faster than the richer industrial countries in the European core.

We owe to the pioneer work of Clark (1940) and Kuznets (1966) the important insight that modern economic growth is characterised by structural change of a non-random and systematic character. None of the previous globalisations had led to major, progressive and lasting structural transformations in any of the participating economies. The first country to modernise and industrialise was, of course, Britain. A highly stylised story of the structural transformation of the British economy during the period of transition to modern economic growth could be told along the following lines. There was a thriving worldwide market for cotton textiles – the only truly global commodity at that time – and India was the major supplier. The British government had imposed barriers on the importation of Indian cotton textiles for domestic consumption in 1701 (though the importation of calicos was permitted for re-export).[4] The aim of the British government was to keep protecting the domestic market to encourage the substitution of Indian cotton textiles by domestic production and to corner as large a share of the world market as possible. In this view – a view with which we concur – the mechanisation of cotton textiles production took place in response to challenges posed by Indian cotton textiles, in wanting to imitate the vibrancy, finesse and quality of these textiles, and to out-compete the Indian producers in both the domestic and world markets. The most forceful advocate of this view has been Parthasarathi (2011). We shall elaborate on this view as well as the competing views on the mechanisation of cotton textile manufacturing in due course (in Chapter 3). We note here, however, that in the case of the cotton textile technology, the technology, in a very important sense, could be said to have been embodied in the product itself, and that the machines that led to the mechanisation of production in the industry were pretty "basic", and their developments required no great conceptual leaps.

The other manufacturing of importance was metalwares. But in the eighteenth century most of the output of metalwares had been the product of handicraft industries. And in the case of the iron industry, it took a "hundred years for the industry to transform itself from a small producer at a high cost in the early eighteenth century to becoming the leading supplier of iron product in the world market by 1820". For a long time when the domestic supply of iron was inadequate to meet the domestic demand, the gap between the two was met by imports from Sweden and, increasingly in the second half of the eighteenth century from Russia (as late as 1750, more than 65 per cent of the British bar iron was imported). To encourage import substitution, the government had levied duties on imported iron, and the rising duties and the gap between the domestic supply and demand then provided the needed incentive for increasing production. This was achieved by switching from charcoal fuel to coal fuel in smelting iron. The industry subsequently came to rely on export markets for its expansion. While the customer base changed over time, increasingly Britain's iron industry "could only enlarge her export markets, especially after 1850, by diverting her incremental deliveries from her closest continental competitors, namely Belgium, France and Germany, to less developed countries such as Russia and India". The product mix of British iron exports also shifted "towards the lower stages of production from bar iron to pig iron".[5]

Meanwhile, there had been the transfer of wealth taking place from India to Britain from the mid-eighteenth century onwards, which, among many other things, made possible foreign investment by the British at this early stage (more on this in Chapter 2). Both the visible and invisible incomes increased greatly as a result of international involvements. Returns from foreign investment became important from an early stage. The share of modern (i.e., the mechanised and factory based as opposed to household based) manufacturing and modern services in national income increased. However, the share of manufacturing in employment and output did not become significant until well into the 1820s. Britain was a supplier of services before she became the workshop of the world (see Cain and Hopkins 2001). The share of urban to total population increased. In due course, agricultural productivity and output also increased in response to increased demand for the produce of the agricultural sector from the urban areas and because of the availability of better and cheaper inputs from, and services provided by, the urban areas to the agricultural sector (more on this below). There was an increase in rural to urban migration. The structural transformation of the economy had occurred, profoundly influenced by Britain's interactions with the outside world, and per capita income increased noticeably from the 1830s or so even as population increased.

In the discussion above, we have emphasised the role of Britain's interactions with the outside world in bringing about the structural transformations. Those who, by contrast, wish to give prominence to factors such as religion, culture or institutions would have to contend with the fact that, according to the recently reconstructed historical GDP data, as we have already noted, Britain – after a brief spurt in its GDP per capita growth during the period 1650s to the 1690s (and this following nearly two and a half centuries of near stagnant GDP/capita) – was again returning to stagnant growth or worse, with all of the GDP/capita growth of the late seventeenth century petering out before the 1780s. There was also a substantial decline in agricultural output per capita.[6] Allen's (1999, 2004, 2005) data show a decrease in agricultural output per capita of 33 per cent in 1750–1800; Clark's (2010, 2017) estimates show an even greater decline of over 60 per cent during this period. British agriculture was clearly losing the battle to keep pace with population growth. In these circumstances, it is difficult to see how, in the absence of the transfer of wealth from India and increased international involvements, true – as opposed to proto – industrialisation and modern economic growth could have established themselves in Britain by the early decades of the nineteenth century.

The British experience would also seem to go against the widely held view that agricultural development is in some sense a pre-requisite to industrial development and that it is agriculture which must necessarily provide resources for industrialisation. Instead, the

British experience would seem to have been one of industrialisation (profoundly influenced as that was by overseas involvements) first and then agricultural transformations following in its wake. The high rate of growth of agricultural productivity which ultimately overcame the Malthusian problem in Britain was a nineteenth – and not an eighteenth century – phenomenon. So far as the inter-sectoral flow of funds between agriculture and industry is concerned, it also now appears highly likely that there probably was a net inflow of funds towards rather than away from the agricultural sector. There also does not seem to be conclusive evidence that agriculture could and did release cheap labour for the newly emerging industries in England (see, among others, Sinha 1984).

The view that economic modernisation follows a natural process of evolution, with agricultural development coming first and providing the precondition for industrial revolution, is, of course, a highly respected one with a long tradition, whose root can be traced to Ricardo (1817) and which, in our time, underlies the construction of all dual economy models. As is well known, Lewis (1954, 1958) presents a two-sector model to investigate the expansion of the capitalistic or industrial sector as it is nourished by supplies of cheap labour from the subsistence or agricultural sector. Lewis (1954) stressed a labour surplus rather than an agricultural surplus. It would appear, however, that agricultural output also has to increase if the mechanism that he describes is not to grind to a halt. As he wrote, "if we postulate that the capitalistic sector is not producing food, we must either postulate that the subsistence sector is increasing its output, or else conclude that the expansion of the capitalistic sector will be brought to an end through adverse terms of trade eating into profits". It was, however, Ranis and Fei (1961), in their subsequent elaboration and extension of the Lewis model, who clearly brought out the importance of the agricultural output in initiating and sustaining the process of capital accumulation in the context of the dual economy models.

However, in a fundamental sense, the two-sector models would appear to be less than completely equipped to deal with the question of the agriculture-industry relationship; for even at the dawn of history people did not devote all of their time to exclusively producing food – they also simultaneously produced other goods and services and engaged in other activities. In other words, there always was an informal sector in today's terminology (informal sector is defined to include proto-industrial as well as traditional services and subsistence activities), and any model of development must, therefore, incorporate these people and activities into the analysis in an essential way. Once this is done, one can tell a story clearly quite different from those of the dual economy models, for is it not much more likely that some of these informal activities transform themselves into "formal" modes of production; that the formal/modern sector for its growth does not have to rely on the rural sector for labour or for additional food, but that, instead, as the formal sector grows, it helps bring about transformation in both the rural and the informal sectors? For a three-sector model of development, which systematically incorporates an informal sector, see Bhattacharya (2024).

While the structural transformation in favour of modern manufacturing and services was well established in Britain by the early 1830s or so, it took a while for the continental countries and the USA to undergo structural transformation of their economies. "Continental Europe was little if at all more urbanised in 1800 than in 1600, and indeed that it is possible that there was no significant change between 1400 and 1800" (E. A. Wrigley 2004, quoted by Malanima 2021). The share of manufacturing in national income remained quite small in these countries well into the 1860s. The growth of these countries was profoundly influenced by British policies and actions, based on her Indian foundation. It was indeed important for modern growth that growth did spread to these countries, for while in theory it may be possible to visualise scenarios where modern economic growth takes place in isolation in one country and is sustained there and does not peter out, in practice it is unlikely that modern economic growth could have been sustained in Britain (a small country on the periphery of Europe) unless modern economic growth had also spread to at least a few other countries within a relatively short period of time, as indeed it did. There cannot be just only one country which grows while other countries remain backward for any meaningful growth to be sustainable for long. We shall discuss the consequences of British Indian connections for the development of these countries in some detail in due course (Chapters 2 and 3).

But clearly, there were many other important events occurring in the world economy before the British East India Company (EIC) gained the political control of Bengal – the richest province in India – after the Battle of Plassey in 1757 and then went on to colonise the rest of India from this base. In particular, the "discovery" of America by Columbus in 1492 and the finding of the sea route to the Indies via the

Cape of Good Hope by Vasco da Gama's voyage of 1497–1499 (one should also probably include here the circumnavigation of the globe by Magellan's expedition of 1519–1522) are widely regarded as being among the most significant events in world history. The discovery of America, besides leading to the destruction of its people, also led to the extraction of silver from the Mexican and Peruvian mines in the sixteenth and seventeenth centuries and which added hugely to the stock of silver in circulation (silver being the base for currency in most monetised societies at that time). The discovery of America also led to the Atlantic slave trade to provide the labour needed in areas made empty of people by European diseases (to which the Native Americans had no immunity) and by the cruelty of the Spanish settlers. Slaves were also to be imported to grow cash crops on a wider scale in North America, Brazil, Cuba and various islands in the West Indies.

A number of scholars have forcefully argued that both the increased availability of silver and the Atlantic slave trade made major contributions to European growth and the rise of Europe (see, among others, Inikori 2002; Frank 1998; Acemoglu et al. 2005; Williams 1944). Both contributed to major expansions in international trade. We acknowledge that these were very important events, but how important these events were in the context of the emergence of modern economic growth (which first manifested itself in Britain in the late eighteenth/early nineteenth century) remains, we believe, an open question. Could they have necessarily led to the emergence of modern growth in the absence of the British control of India? Or was the British control of India a necessary condition for the rise of Britain and Europe and the emergence of the first truly globalised world economy? By the very nature of historical problems, there cannot, of course, be a definite or definitive answer to this question, but only one based on balance of probabilities and trying to establish relative scales of importance. We shall try to present arguments to the effect that it was the British control of India that was predominantly responsible for the rise of Europe and the emergence of modern economic growth.

The plan of the rest of the book is as follows. Chapter 2 discusses how the British control of India put Britain at the apex of the world economy and how it was the British policies and actions – based on her Indian foundation – that led not only to the great divergence – i.e., the divergence in income between the Occident and Orient – but also to the globalisation of the nineteenth century, a globalisation very different from the previous globalisations in history.

Chapter 3 looks at technological innovations. Technological innovations are the key to long-term economic growth. Chapter 3 argues that the technological innovations of the nineteenth century were embedded in the nineteenth-century globalisation process, and it is this which ensured that growth and innovations would not peter out this time (as they had done after various "efflorescences" in history).

Chapter 4 considers the role of both the increased circulation of silver (following the extraction of silver from the Mexican and Peruvian mines in the sixteenth and seventeenth centuries) as well as that of the Atlantic slave trade. While these were clearly important events, it is argued that it is unlikely that either of these events set up a mechanism for growth and technological innovations to be a continuing process.

Chapter 5 offers some concluding observations. Each of the Chapters 2 to 4 contains a brief introduction to that chapter.

Notes

1 See, among others, Bolt and van Zanden (2014); van Zanden and van Leeuwen (2012); Broadberry et al. (2015) and Broadberry, Guan and Li (2018).

2 Indeed, it would appear that, according to recently reconstructed historical GDP data, "no large region of Europe prior to 1780 had yet been able to significantly surpass the income per capita achieved by Renaissance northern Italy in 1450" (Goldstone 2015, p. 66).

3 For discussions of these "globalisations", see, among others, Abu-Lughod (1989), Frankopan (2015) and Flynn and Giraldez (2008).

4 A more comprehensive ban was enacted in 1721. See the discussion on p. 66 below.

5 See Fremdling (2000).

6 It is true that there has been a great deal of debate regarding the progress in productivity and output in English/British agriculture in the eighteenth century (Overton 1996; Allen 1999, 2000, 2005; Clark 2010, 2017; Broadberry et al. 2015; Kelley and O'Grada 2013). No agricultural statistics were produced at the national level before 1866. So there is some uncertainty regarding the estimates of agricultural output before this time. However, and as Goldstone (2015) has pointed out, the findings of studies on agricultural output and productivity could profitably be read in conjunction with information on calorie consumption and heights, and these would appear to support the conclusions regarding a decline in per capita agricultural output during the period mentioned. See Goldstone (2015, pp. 30–31).

References

Abu-Lughod, J. (1989), *Before European Hegemony*, New York: Oxford University Press.

Acemoglu, D., Johnson, S. and Robinson, J. (2005), "The rise of Europe: Atlantic trade, institutional change, and economic growth", *American Economic Review*, Vol. 95, pp. 546–579.

Allen, R. C. (1999), "Tracking the agricultural revolution in England", *Economic History Review*, Vol. 52, pp. 209–235.

Allen, R. C. (2000), "Economic structure, and agricultural productivity in Europe, 1300–1800", *European Review of Economic History*, Vol. 3, pp. 1–25.

Allen, R. C. (2004), "Agriculture during the industrial revolution, 1700–1850" in Floud, R. and Johnsons, P. (eds.), *The Cambridge Economic History of Modern Britain*, Vol. 1, Cambridge: Cambridge University Press, pp. 96–116.

Allen, R. C. (2005), "English and Welsh agriculture, 1300–1850: Output, inputs, and income", Economics Working Paper, Nuffield College, Oxford University.

Bhattacharya, P. (2024), *Informal Sector in Economic Development: An Analytical Foundation*, London: Palgrave Macmillan.

Bolt, J. and van Zanden, J. L. (2014), "The Maddison project: Collaborative research on historical national accounts", *Economic History Review*, Vol. 67, pp. 627–651.

Broadberry, S., Campbell, B., Klein, A., Overton, M. and van Leeuwen, B. (2015), *British Economic Growth, 1270–1870*, Cambridge: Cambridge University Press.

Broadberry, S., Guan, H. and Li, D. (2018), "China, Europe and great divergence: A study in historical national accounting", *Journal of Economic History*, Vol. 78, pp. 955–1000.

Cain, P. J. and Hopkins, A. G. (2001), *British Imperialism: 1688–2000*. London: Routledge.

Clark, C. (1940), *Conditions of Economic Progress*, London: Macmillan.

Clark, G. (2010), "Long march" in Field, A. J. (ed.), *Research in Economic History*, Leeds: Emerald Group Publishing, pp. 51–140.

Clark, G. (2017), "Growth or stagnation? Farming in England, 1200–1800", *Economic History Review*, Vol. 70, pp. 1–27.

Crafts, N. (1985), *British Economic Growth During the Industrial Revolution*, Oxford: Oxford University Press.

Crafts, N. and Harley, C. (1992), "Output growth and the British Industrial Revolution: A restatement of the Crafts-Harley view", *Economic History Review*, Vol. 45, No. 4, pp. 703–730.

Flynn, D. O. and Giraldez, O. (2008), "Born again: Globalisation's sixteenth-century origins", *Pacific Economic Review*, Vol. 3, pp. 359–387.

Frank, A. G. (1998), *Reorient: Global Economy in the Asian Age*, Berkeley: University of California Press.

Frankopan, P. (2015), *The Silk Roads: A New History of the World*, London: Bloomsbury.

Fremdling, R. (2000), "Transfer patterns of British technology to the Continent: The case of the iron industry", *European Review of Economic History*, Vol. 4, pp. 195–222.

Goldstone, J. A. (2002), "Efflorescences and economic growth in world history: Rethinking the 'Rise of the West' and the industrial revolution", *Journal of World History*, Vol. 13, pp. 323–389.

Goldstone, J. A. (2015), "The great and little divergence: Where lies the true onset of modern economic growth?", Working Paper. Available at SSRN: https://ssrn.com/abstract=2599287.

Goldstone, J. A. (2021), "Why understanding the timing of divergence matters", *Journal of Global History*, Vol. 16, pp. 309–314.

Inikori, J. E. (2002), *Africans and the Industrial Revolution in England: A Study in International Trade and Economic Development*, Cambridge: Cambridge University Press.

Kelly, M. and O'Grada, C. (2013), "Numerare est errate: Agricultural output and food supply in England before and during the industrial revolution", *Journal of Economic History*, Vol. 73, pp. 1132–1163.

Kuznets, S. (1966), *Modern Economic Growth*, New Haven: Yale University Press.

Lewis, W. A. (1954), "Economic development with unlimited supplies of labour", *The Manchester School*, Vol. 22, pp. 139–191.

Lewis, W. A. (1958), "Unlimited labour: Further notes", *The Manchester School*, Vol. 26, pp. 1–32.

Malanima, P. (2021), "Past growth: Pre-modern and modern", *Journal of Global History*, Vol. 16, pp. 301–308.

Overton, M. (1996), *Agricultural Revolution in England: The Transformation of the Agrarian Economy 1500–1850*, Cambridge: Cambridge University Press.

Parthasarathi, P. (2011), *Why Europe Grew Rich and Asia Did Not: Global Economic Divergence, 1600–1850*, Cambridge: Cambridge University Press.

Ranis, G. and Fei, J. (1961), "A theory of economic development", *American Economic Review*, Vol. LI, No. 4, pp. 533–565.

Ricardo, D. (1817), *The Principles of Political Economy and Taxation*, Sraffa, P. (ed.) (1951), Cambridge: Cambridge University Press.

Sinha, R. (1984), "Challenging conventional wisdom in agricultural development", *Development Policy Review: The Journal of the Overseas Development Institute*, Vol. 2, pp. 59–77.

van Zanden, J. and van Leeuwen, B. (2012), "Persistent but not consistent: The growth of national income in Holland, 1347–1807", *Explorations in Economic History*, Vol. 49, pp. 119–130.

Williams, E. (1944), *Capitalism and Slavery*, Chapel Hill: University of North Carolina Press.

Wrigley, E. A. (2004), "Urban growth in early modern Europe" in Wrigley, E. A. (ed.), *Poverty, Progress and Population*, Cambridge: Cambridge University Press.

2 India in the rise of Britain and Europe

Convergence and great divergence

Introduction

"Europe" and European offshoots have been the dominant influences in the world economy until very recently. And while there may be a shift currently under way towards Asia, Europe and European offshoots still have per capita incomes much higher than those in China and India (with India's per capita income being considerably lower than that of China). The purpose of this chapter is to examine the role of the British control of India in the so-called "great divergence" – the long-term divergence in growth, productivity and living standards between the Occident and Orient – as well as in the convergence in incomes within the Atlantic economy. This last refers to the fact that in the late nineteenth century[1] many "poor countries in the European periphery tended to grow faster than the rich industrial leaders at the European centre, and often even faster than the labour-scarce countries overseas in the New World" (Aghion and Williamson 1999, p. 105), and there was a convergence in living standards within this group of countries in the Atlantic world[2] (even as there was a divergence in income between the Occident and Orient).

As is well known, a number of explanations have been put forward to explain the rise and dominance of Europe. The main focus of most of these explanations has primarily been on the period between 1500 and 1800. One group of explanations has looked at factors internal to Europe, with various protagonists arguing variously, for example, that "western religion, culture or institutions" were uniquely excellent and that any of or all of these together explain the rise and dominance of Europe.[3] However, as Pomeranz (2000, p. 16) has pointed out, a major problem with these Europe-centred stories is that "there is

DOI: 10.4324/9781003715368-2

little to suggest that Western Europe's economy had decisive advantage before 1800, either in its capital stock or economic institutions" compared to those in (many other) comparable regions in Asia (the Yangste delta in China, Kanto plain in Japan or Gujarat in India).

Another group of explanations has focused on various forms of colonial extraction (including on the interactions between colonial extraction and domestic institutions).[4] In an important contribution, Pomeranz went beyond the usual arguments in this context to argue that access to coal and the "ghost acreage" that Europe derived from the New World were of critical importance. "The slave trade and other features of European colonial systems" in the New World "enabled Europe to exchange an ever-growing volume of manufactured exports for an ever-growing volume of land-intensive products" (Pomeranz 2000, p. 20). Together, coal and the New World allowed Europe to grow along resource-intensive, labour-saving paths (in contrast to the core of East Asia's economy which was forced along labour-intensive, resource-saving paths that led to an ecological impasse).

It has also been argued that the Industrial Revolution (IR), founded as it was on labour-saving mechanical technology, was more likely to take off in areas where labour was relatively more expensive: see, among others, Habakkuk (1962), Allen (2009) and Rosenthal and Wong (2011). Allen, in particular, has argued that the IR was the result of Britain's high-wage economy. It is also, of course, possible to argue that capital-using, labour-saving innovations are more likely to appear if the supply of capital increases. Indeed, we shall argue below that this is precisely what happened in Britain at the time of the IR due to the transfer of wealth from India to Britain. We shall also argue that India made Britain a more saving and investing country.

There have also been debates about when exactly the so-called "great divergence" started. Pomeranz thought that the divergence started around 1800, while Broadberry (2013) has argued that it started around 1500; Shui and Keller (2007) believe that China and the West were at similar levels of development around 1800, while Parthasaathi (2011) thinks that India was at par with the West until 1750 or so. Goldstone (2015) too argues in favour of a later start to the great divergence, and the recently reconstructed historical GDP data for a number of countries, as we noted in the last chapter, would seem to support the view of a later start. It is also worth bearing in mind that little if any real per capita growth can be discerned in Britain before 1830. Also, that European industrialisation was very limited before 1860.

The key consideration here, however, as Mokyr (2003) has pointed out, is that growth was sustained in Western Europe after the IR, instead of petering out, as in the previous episodes of growth, and that the gap in income between Western Europe and Asia had become huge by 1900. This places a particular onus of responsibility for historical change in the period after 1750 or so. Mokyr (2005) has argued that technological development played the critical role here. Sustained technological progress was the key to the "great divergence", and Britain was the leader in economic applications of new technology. According to Mokyr, the West produced useful knowledge at the time of the IR, and conditions were right for the continued growth of this useful knowledge. To quote Mokyr, "the technological breakthroughs of the period prepared the ground for the economic transformation that made the difference between the West and the Rest" (Mokyr 2005, p. 19).

In this context, it should first be noted, as Mokyr himself acknowledges, that pure science itself played very little role in economic development until towards the end of the nineteenth century. Instead, it is technological developments which were the important influences. But then technological developments do not take place in a vacuum; they take place in pursuance of profits and when people see opportunities for rewards from innovating. When an economy is an expansive frame and/or undergoing major structural changes, challenges and opportunities open up for successful technological advances to take place. (Subsequently, these technological developments themselves may, of course, lead to further profit opportunities and technological advances). We shall discuss the question of technological advances in the context of the IR in the next chapter.

It will be a major argument of this chapter that the British advances in India from the mid-eighteenth century onwards released expansive forces for the British economy and subsequently for European economies and their development. The economic destiny of Europe from the late eighteenth century was shaped by the early industrialisation in Britain which then spread to a few countries on the European continent (and then to the USA). Britain was at the apex of the world economy throughout most of the nineteenth century. It will be argued that the emergence of Britain as the apex economic and political power depended on her control over India. This control of India then enabled

Britain to pursue a set of policies that were of critical importance both for the convergence in incomes within the Atlantic economy and for the "rise of Europe". It is this which made the difference between the West and the Rest in the nineteenth century. It will also be argued that the globalisation process of the nineteenth century rested on Britain's Indian foundation. The thesis advanced here can be viewed, depending on one's prior position, as being either complementary to or alternative to the views of many of the protagonists of the divergence debate referred to above.

India's direct contributions to the British economic development

This section focuses on India's direct contributions to the British economic development. These can be usefully discussed under the following headings: the transfer of wealth from India to Britain; the role of the Indian Army in furthering British economic, military and political interests; the role of India as a "captive" market for British goods; the role of India's China trade in furthering British economic development and global influence; and last, but not the least, the role of India as a source of labour for other British tropical colonies. We briefly elaborate on each of these contributions below.

Transfer of wealth from India

Adam Smith referred to the EIC as the body "for the appointment of plunderers of India".[5] Extortion and plunder were common as the Company acquired political strength in parts of southern India and dominance over Bengal. Huge amounts of wealth flowed into the pockets of the Company servants, from "presents", from collusive contracts with officials of Indian rulers, and through the pressures that were exerted to make internal trade favourable to the English buyer or seller. And after 1765 when the Company acquired from the Mughal Emperor the cession of the *diwani* (the management and collection of the revenue) of Bengal, this solved the problem of the export of bullion from Great Britain (to obtain Indian goods): it paid for the merchandise bought by the EIC. The Company, in other words, used Indian revenue to buy goods in India (and later in China) to be exported to Britain. The aim essentially was to transfer wealth from India to Britain.

There have been several estimates of the drain of wealth from India to Britain. Furber (1948, p. 304) set out his formulation of the drain as follows: "the only true drain resulting from contact with the West was the excess of exports from India for which there was no equivalent import". Furber estimated this drain to have been £11.8 million over the period 1783–1792 (at current prices), i.e., an average of £1.3 million per annum. Other estimates of this drain include Maddison's (1971) estimate of £100 million for the period 1757–1815; Hamilton's (1919) and Sinha's (1956) estimates of £34.5 million and £38.4 million, respectively, for the same period of 1757–1780; Burke's (1981) estimate of £1 million per year for the four years ending 1780; and Habib's (1974) estimate of well over £2 million for 1789–1790. A rigorous recent estimate is that by Cuenca Esteban (2001) for the period 1772–1820 whose figures show the "arguably minimum transfer" from India to Britain – in the balance of payments sense – reaching a peak of £1.01 million annually in 1784–1792.

What were the effects of this drain from India on the British economy? A major effect would appear to have been that this Indian transfer enabled Britain to liquidate its foreign debt in critical years before the French wars. The transfer also helped Britain to generate a current account surplus necessary for foreign investment. There had been a growing Dutch investment in British government (and other British) stocks. "This Dutch investment had grown rapidly in each of the eighteenth-century wars down to 1763, did not grow at all in the war of 1776–83, and most importantly this debt of £25–30 million was rapidly liquidated in a few years after 1783". Davis (1978, p. 55) was the first to suggest that "Indian wealth supplied the funds that bought national debt back from the Dutch and others, first and temporarily in the interval of peace between 1763 and 1774, and finally after 1783, leaving Britain nearly free from overseas indebtedness when it came to face the great French wars from 1793". By 1800, it is believed that Britain had an external surplus of £10 million.[6] Cuenca Esteban's (2001) reconstruction of British Balance of Payments over the period 1772–1820 supported Davis by showing that without the Indian transfers, Britain would have required mounting foreign borrowing during this period to seemingly unsustainable levels after 1809. In Cuenca Esteban's reconstruction "the gap between 'actual' debts or credits abroad and 'counterfactual' foreign indebtedness[7] widens exponentially from £87 million in 1802 to £114 million by 1807, and to £170 million by 1815" (Cuenca Esteban 2001, pp. 67–68).

If we remember that during the eighteenth-century wars, Britain followed a "blue-water" strategy – a strategy which involved giving huge subsidies to allies on the continent to fight land wars against the French, while the Royal Navy protected the British Isles from invasion and harassed French trade – it would appear that Cuenca Esteban was right to conclude that "without the accumulated credits from India transfers since 1757, Britain's financing of land warfare during the French wars would have been compromised" (Cuenca Esteban 2001, p. 58).

In a subsequent paper, Cuenca Esteban (2007) expanded his previous work to include *the re-export of Indian goods from Britain.* British trade inflows from re-exports of Indian commodities alone most frequently doubled, and at times tripled, those arising from net Indian transfers including government flows. As Esteban says, "the total net credit on 'trade and services excluding India' could not have sustained Britain's war expenses in Continental Europe since 1793" (Cuenca Esteban 2007, p. 167).

It should also be noted in this context that Esteban's estimates were based on trade statistics, but clearly a large part of the Indian wealth came clandestinely or in the form of treasures and diamonds that did not appear in the trade statistics. For one, there were war indemnity and forced loans; Tipu alone paid £3.5 million in coins and bullions to the Company at the end of the war in 1792 (Siddiqi 1995, p. 19). For another, as already mentioned, there were tributes and "presents" by the princely states. It is thus clear that the drain of wealth from India can only have been much higher than any estimates based on the trade statistics alone.

Be that as it may, as we have noted, Britain is believed to have had an external surplus of £10 million by 1800. It is difficult to see how this surplus would have appeared without the Indian transfer. Britain "passed from being a debtor to being a creditor nation", and Cuenca Esteban's estimates place the decisive turning point in the late 1790s. "In subsequent years, British net gains on trade and services would have compounded, for the first time, with positive returns on investment" (Cuenca Esteban 2007, p. 168).[8]

Indian transfer would thus appear to have been making possible foreign investment by the British as early as the 1790s. This was important for domestic economic stability, for from the mid-1820s, in particular, Britain came to depend upon rapidly increasing returns on earlier investment (in Europe, North America and the Middle East) to provide a continued current account surplus and to hold imports of raw materials at a level that would maintain domestic employment (Cain and Hopkins 2001, p. 91). As will be discussed below, the British invested heavily in foreign countries throughout the nineteenth century, and this had profound significance for the evolution of both the British and the world economy. The genesis of the British foreign investment in the nineteenth century can thus be seen to lie in the transfer of wealth from India to Britain in the early years of the Company rule. Later too, as the nineteenth century progressed, the Indian connection would prove vital for the continued foreign investment by the British, as India became a major market for British exports and as India continued to contribute massively to income from services. These will be discussed in due course.

Indian transfer and control of India also – in a number of different ways – made Britain a more saving and investing country. Most of the imports from India during this period, as it were, were obtained more or less free.[9] So some of the income generated domestically in Britain which would have been spent on imported goods otherwise could now be saved, and some of the savings exported as capital. Further, the EIC's control of India directly generated income for the government (in the form of taxes and customs revenues) as well as for the members of the public. As the Company used more and more of the Indian revenue to purchase goods for export to Britain, both directly and via China (India's China trade will be discussed below), so the Company's annual payments of customs duties in London rose sharply. The Company, for example, was able to make payments of over £1 million on customs and tea duties in 1786/1787 alone. This rose to £3 million a year during the 1820s, mainly in the form of tea duties[10] (more on this below).

So the tax revenue was higher as a result of the Indian connection. This tax revenue was in a very important sense generated because the EIC had control over the Indian revenue. It is also clear that the government expenditure too would have had to have been very much higher without the control of India, for the Indian revenue, as we shall see, paid for a large part of the British army, British merchant ships and sailors, and all of the Indian Army, all of which furthered British trade and commerce. So the control over India had positive impacts on both the public and private savings.

Finally, we may refer here to the argument that was advanced by O'Brien (1982) regarding the contribution of commerce with the periphery to aggregate capital accumulation in Britain. O'Brien provided an estimate of profits accruing to British shipping firms, bankers and commissioning agencies, and insurance companies from their involvement in trade with the less developed regions of the world during the late eighteenth century (1784–1786 to be precise). He put the figure at approximately £5.6 million. He relied on Davis (1978) for his figures that imports from the periphery were about £10.50 million during this period. Total gross investment during the period was £10.30 million. During this period, the aggregate savings rate was between 12 and 14 per cent; assuming that the savings rate from these profit incomes was 30 per cent, O'Brien concluded that the contribution of these profits (resulting from trade with the periphery) to aggregate capital accumulation would be only about 15 per cent or so, and he concluded that "for the economic growth of the core, the periphery was peripheral" (O'Brien 1982, p. 12). Inikori (2002) has subsequently suggested that imports from the periphery around 1800 were about double O'Brien's estimate. More importantly, in the context of the present discussion, O'Brien completely missed the point that of the £10.50 million of imports from the periphery during 1784–1786 that he cites (from Davis), nearly 50 per cent (£4,952 million according to Davis' calculations) came from Asia, most of which were bought with the Indian revenue directly or indirectly. In other words, O'Brien ignored the transfer of wealth from India to Britain. He also ignored the customs and tea duties that resulted from the control of India. If the transfer of wealth from India is added to O'Brien's estimates of profits from trade with the periphery, the contribution of periphery to aggregate capital accumulation in Britain during this period, using his methodology, could be, depending on one's assumptions, as high as 70 per cent or even higher. In these terms alone, the periphery, instead of being peripheral, would appear to have been central to the British economy and economic development during this period.

The contributions of the Indian Army

Seizure of the India revenue made it possible for Britain to build up in India one of the largest standing armies in the world. Indian taxpayers paid for the expenses not only of the Indian troops, but also of regiments and detachments from the British regular army that served in India.

As early as 1766, the Company had maintained an army of 32,379 soldiers, of whom 9,443 were Europeans of various nationalities (Richards 2006, p. 25). By 1781, the army had quadrupled in size to 124,000, of whom 23,000 were Europeans – many of the latter were British Royal Army troops. In 1847 about 33,000 of the 140,000 British regular army troops were stationed in India. By 1851, the pre-Rebellion army in India totalled 289,529, of whom 49,408 were British regular troops. After the Rebellion, the Indian sepoy was at no time to outnumber British troops in the subcontinent by more than two to one, but this was not always adhered to. In 1881, the Indian Army numbered 69,647 British troops and 125,000 sepoys, compared with British and Irish forces at home of 65,809 and 25,353, respectively. In other words, there were more British troops stationed in India at Indian taxpayers' expenses than British troops maintained in Britain at British taxpayers' expenses.

The Indian Army was used not only to pacify the subcontinent itself, but after 1790 it was increasingly employed to forward British interests elsewhere which directly or indirectly protected Britain's commercial interests and furthered British trade and influences. The campaign against the French in Egypt in 1789 and the seizure of the Cape of Good Hope in 1795 and 1806 anticipated what was to come. The lucrative timber trade was forwarded by the defeats of Burma (1824–1826 and 1852). In the 1840s and 1850s, the intervention of the Indian Army in China widened the entrée of British trade into valuable Far Eastern markets. The ambit of Indian power is described by the movement of her troops: to, as already mentioned, China in 1839, 1856, 1859 and 1909 (the last during the Boxer Rebellion); to Persia in 1856, to Ethiopia and Singapore in 1867, to Hong Kong in 1868, to Malaya in 1875, to Malta in 1878, to Afghanistan in 1838 and then again in 1878, to Egypt in 1882, to Burma in 1885, to Nayasa in 1893, to the Sudan and Uganda in 1896, South Africa in 1899 and Tibet in 1903. Indian taxpayers paid not only the expenses of both Indian and British troops in India, but also some fractions of the costs of Indian and British troops used in these imperial adventures. The Indian Army provided the means of intimidating and, if needed, "crushing the resistance of Asiatic rulers who obstructed British influence and trade". As Robinson and Gallagher put it, "Between them, the Sepoys and the Royal Navy guarded the commercial empire throughout the eastern seas and the Pacific" (Robinson and Gallagher 1961, p. 13).

The story is not complete without putting the annual expenditure of the British Army in the wider context of the total annual expenditure of the United Kingdom. Wong (1998) has provided an analysis of the composition of the UK government expenditure during the period 1835 to 1860.[11] The average annual UK government expenditure during the period was £59.25 million. The largest component of this expenditure was the payment of interest on the public debt, amounting to an average of £28.9 million per year. The second largest item of expenditure was the expenditure on "Army and ordnance" at £10.5 million or almost one-fifth of the total UK government expenditure, with the expenditure on the Navy coming third at £7.3 million. Other items of expenditure were very small in comparison (with "Law and justice", for example, coming fourth at £1.92 million). It is obvious that the expenditure on "Army and ordnance" would have to have been very much higher if Britain did not have the control of the Indian revenue, but wanted to maintain the same sort of overseas commitments. The Indian Army, paid for by the Indian revenue, was politically, financially and strategically of immense importance to the British. Without the Indian Army and the Indian base, the penetration of China would have been difficult and the so-called "informal" empire difficult to establish. As has been said, without the Indian Army, Britain would only have been a naval power, with it she became a continental power.

India as a "captive" market for British goods and British trade surplus with India

As the interest income from investment abroad became available to some significant extent from the mid-1820s (see p. 19 above), the need to transfer capital from India by tribute declined. India would now become the cornerstone of the free trade policy to be pursued by the British. A fraction of Home Charges[12] would continue as tribute, but keeping Indian markets open for British goods and generating trade surplus with India would become key British policy goals.

Foreign markets played a very important – some would say, a decisive – role in early British industrial expansion. By the end of the eighteenth century domestic exports accounted for about 13 per cent of the GDP, by the end of the 1870s this had risen to about 22 per cent, and thereafter they averaged between 16 and 20 per cent until the First World War. For the major industries, foreign markets were even more important. The cotton industry exported over half the total value of its output at the beginning of the nineteenth century and almost four-fifths at the end, while the iron and steel industry exported about 40 per cent of its output from the mid-nineteenth century.[13]

India was to become over time an increasingly vital market for British exports, especially for cotton goods. In the early part of the nineteenth century, most of the markets for cotton goods were in the USA and Latin America. As tariffs rose in the USA and Europe after the end of the Napoleonic wars, India began to emerge as a prominent market. "Sales to India were responsible for three-tenths of the increase in cotton exports between 1830 and 1850, by which date the subcontinent absorbed 18.5 per cent of all cotton piece-goods sent abroad" (Cain 1999, p. 34). By 1860, nearly 40 per cent of total British exports consisted of cotton textiles, and India absorbed 40 per cent of Britain's total exports of cotton goods. The British policy in India, however, was aimed not only at keeping Indian markets open for British cotton textiles but also at preventing India's emergence as an export competitor.[14]

The importance of cotton for the British economy and British economic growth should not be underestimated. By 1810 it had overtaken wool to become Britain's single most important source of industrial value-added, a position it retained until the very end of the nineteenth century. It was the largest single industry by a substantial margin. By 1850 there were 331,000 factory workers in cotton spinning and weaving in 1,923 mills. There were about another 150,000 cotton workers outside of factories and a further 31,000 dyers and calico printers.[15] Even as late as 1880, over 80 per cent of the world's cotton exports came from Britain. To Rostow, cotton represented the original leading sector in the first take-off. Without doubt, the captive Indian market was of vital importance for the continued growth of this industry. If India had been an independent country, India in all probability would have protected her own cotton industry. Britain's political control of India was of paramount importance in the context of the growth of the cotton industry in Britain. (Indeed, it will be argued in Chapter 3 that the mechanisation of the cotton textile industry in Britain in the second half of the eighteenth century had taken place in wanting to imitate the vibrancy, colour and finesse of the Indian cotton textiles which had dominated the world market until then, and that the protectionist policies of the British government against the importation of Indian cotton textiles were integral to that process).

India was also an important market for machinery (£4.5 million out of £33.6 million in 1913) and locomotives and railway carriages (£2.2 million out of £7.0 million in 1913).

In 1870, India took nearly one-fifth of total British exports. "Between 1870 and 1913 India rose from third to first place among Britain's export markets".[16] By contrast, India's share of Britain's imports fell to about 10 per cent around the turn of the century. Britain's favourable trade balance with India was hugely important, for India maintained a trading surplus with countries in Asia and Europe (and the USA) that enjoyed surpluses with Britain, and this was to prove to be of great importance for the evolution of the world economy.

Britain, because of her free trade policy (British free trade policy is discussed below), was a major importer of manufactured goods from the new industrial countries, with whom she developed substantial deficits. But she was also the chief exporter of manufactured goods to the less developed countries and had substantial surpluses with them, particularly with India.[17] Without her surplus with India (and to a much lesser extent with China and the Straits Settlements, with her surplus with China and the Straits Settlements also, as we shall see in the next section, resting on her Indian foundation), Britain would not have been able to settle her debts with the new industrial nations and "presumably would have been forced to abandon free trade".[18] The USA and industrial Europe, in particular Germany, were able to continue their policy of tariff protection only because of Britain's surplus with India. Without this Indian surplus, Britain would no longer have been able to subsidise their growth.[19] Indeed, before the First World War "the key to Britain's whole payments pattern lay in India, balancing as she probably did more than two fifths of Britain's total deficits" (Saul 1960).

But how was India able to sustain the massive debt that she had on her transactions with Britain? India's trade deficit with Britain was more than offset by her surpluses with Europe, the USA, and particularly Asia. Europe and America's import of primary products from India far outweighed their export of manufactured goods to India, where British goods were already entrenched. But by far the largest surpluses for India originated from Asia, mainly from China. This surplus with China was of overwhelming importance and was mainly due to the export of opium. India also exported cotton yarn to China, but it was opium that was the dominating item. Ceylon, Thailand and the Straits Settlements also provided useful surpluses for India. The

Straits Settlements, like China, were a victim of the opium trade. Additionally, the Straits Settlements also imported rice from India, to feed their Indian migrant workers, as indeed did Ceylon. (Thailand too imported rice from India). We discuss the magnitude and significance of Indian migrant workers in the section after the next. It is to a discussion of India's China trade that we turn in the next section. As we shall see, India's China trade was of great importance to Britain and the evolution of the world economy in a number of different ways.

India's China trade[20]

The import of tea, in particular, and to a lesser extent, the import of raw silk from China were to become of great importance for the British economy and the British lifestyle in the eighteenth and nineteenth centuries.

The take-off in demand for tea began early in the eighteenth century, with the EIC importing over 2 million pounds of tea between 1713 and 1720. Growth continued to be spectacular in each of the subsequent decades, with imports of 8.9 million pounds in the 1720s, 11.7 million in the 1730s, 20.2 million in the 1740s and 37.4 million in the 1750s.

Up to 1784, tea duties ranged from 75.9 per cent to 127.5 per cent ad valorem and such high duties encouraged smuggling. To undercut the smugglers and to encourage the consumption of "legal" tea, duties on tea were reduced from 119 per cent to 12.5 per cent ad valorem by Pitt's Commutation Act of 1784. The effect was spectacular. In 1784 just under 10 million pounds of tea had been sold, but the amount increased sharply to almost 15 million pounds the following year, and sales topped 20 million pounds in 1795. With minor breaks, the steady increases continued, reaching over 85 million pounds in 1854. Almost all of the tea came from China.[21] Moreover, increasing sales (and sales of better quality tea) meant that government revenue did not suffer greatly in the long run, and pre-1784 levels of revenue income were restored by 1794 before they then rose sharply as progressively higher rates of duty were charged during the wars against France, and rising to 100 per cent and more in the first years of the nineteenth century. The duty was not reduced, however, after the Napoleonic wars.

As already mentioned (p. 19 above), the Company was able to make payments of over £1 million in customs and tea duties in 1786/1787 and upwards of £3 million a year during the 1820s. During the period 1835–1858, tea duty made up an average of 20.95 per cent of the United Kingdom's entire customs revenue or 8.68 per cent of the United Kingdom's gross revenue.[22] The significance of this can also be gauged from another comparative perspective: by noting that the revenue from tea duty alone would have covered two-thirds of the UK government's average annual expenditure on the navy (at £7.3 million) during this period or about half of the average annual expenditure on "Army and ordnance".[23] (See also the discussion on pp. 19–20 above).

In addition to the income from tea sales and contributions to the treasury, tea trade generated large amounts of invisible incomes. Shipping, insurance and other services all generated employment and income. Tea drinking indeed had become a part of the fabric of the society. With milk and sugar added (sugar obtained from the West Indies colonies), tea supplemented the poor diet of factory workers. Not only the factory workers, but all classes of the British society developed the habit of drinking morning and afternoon tea. Tea drinking also had an important influence in reducing the high mortality rates. In England, in the first decades of the eighteenth century, the death rate had risen sharply and exceeded the birth rate. This rise of the death rate historians attribute partly to the growth of drinking cheap gin instead of beer (Trevelyan 1942, pp. 341–344). Gin drinking was encouraged by throwing open the distilling trade and by placing on spirits far too light a tax. It was only as the appalling social consequences of drinking gin – so eloquently captured in Hogarth's delineation of the "horror of Gin lane" contrasted with the "prosperous Beer street" – became apparent that the Parliament moved in 1751 to tax the spirits highly and undertook policies to limit the consumption of gin. Also, after the middle of the century, tea drinking became a strong rival to alcohol consumption in all classes, and after 1780 "the death rate went down by leaps and bounds". While this decline of the death rate was also due to many other factors, a change in drinking habits did play its part.

Apart from tea, the other major item imported from China was the raw silk. By the mid-nineteenth century, the imported Chinese raw silk accounted for a little over half of all the raw silks imported into the United Kingdom. A significant proportion of the raw silk imported was re-exported, mainly to Continental Europe and the Americas. (For example, in 1857 the United Kingdom bought nearly £7 million worth of silk from China, 18 per cent of which was re-exported).[24]

The China trade was clearly important for the British economy. At first Britain struggled to maintain the trade as China would accept only silver as payment, and this was viewed with great concern in this age of mercantilism. After the conquest of Bengal, however, a part of the Bengal revenue could now be used to cover the purchases of Chinese goods at Canton. EIC bought raw cotton in India (with the Indian revenue) to export to China and for a period also remitted silver to China from India. Most importantly, however, opium grown in Bengal became the source of what was to prove the Company's most profitable means of financing the lucrative Chinese tea trade. The Company assumed monopoly rights for the purchase of opium in 1773. State-licensed peasant farmers in relatively small areas in Bengal and Bihar grew opium for a fixed price for the government. Nearly all of the opium grown was exported to China, with some going to the Straits Settlements.

When in 1800 the Emperor of China issued an edict prohibiting the importation of opium, the EIC – to continue the trade – initiated the practice of publicly auctioning the Bengal opium in Calcutta to private traders, who then smuggled it to Canton, obtained silver from the Chinese, handed them to the EIC to purchase Chinese goods and to use the surplus silver elsewhere, and in return obtained bills of exchange from the EIC payable in London or in India. Later, "significant revenue was also derived from levying charges after the establishment of the Malwa Opium Agency in 1823, on the so-called Malwa opium, which was grown in the independent princely states of central India but passed through British territory at Bombay", whence it was smuggled to China (Wong 1998, p. 390).

Often, the value of opium imported into China by private British traders was considerably higher than the total value of the two major exports, tea and silk. For example, in 1833–1834, $11,618,716 worth of opium was smuggled into China, while the value of the two exports amounted to only $4,141,753 (see Wong, p. 374). Since the Company could not use all the surplus silver, it resorted to smuggling the precious metal out of China against a Chinese prohibition. In 1839, China enforced its prohibition of the importation of opium by destroying at Canton a large quantity of opium confiscated from British merchants. The British responded by sending a large contingent of the Indian Army. Two opium wars followed (first in 1839–1842, the second in 1856–1860). The upshot was that China was opened up for trade, a regime of fixed tariffs was imposed upon the Chinese, Hong Kong was ceded to the British and the importation of opium was legalised.

As noted, the Company's China trade generated large trade surpluses for the Company. For example, in the last seven years of the Company's monopoly of China trade – the Company's monopoly of China trade ended in 1834[25] – "while the United Kingdom had an average annual deficit of about £2.76 million in its *bilateral* trade with China, the Chinese had an average annual trade deficit of about £4.59 million with the Company".[26] Later, the Indian surplus with China would increase even further as China was opened up and the quantity of opium exported increased. Indeed, in the 1830s and 1840s opium brought in over 25 per cent of all India's export earnings. In the 1850s this rose to 31 per cent and it held its own at over 20 per cent through the 1860s and 1870s.[27]

From the days of the early EIC government in eighteenth-century Bengal until the end of the Raj, opium revenue ranked in importance just behind land revenue and salt monopoly. Official revenue returns came mainly from either profits or fees on opium exports. As a percentage of the total Indian government revenue, opium revenue rose from 4 per cent in the 1790s to plateau in the period 1850 to 1880 at 16 per cent or over.[28]

Opium was vital for the Company's hold on India. Without the extra revenue provided by opium, the expansion of British rule in India would very probably have been greatly constrained. As the Company continued its expansion in India, its debt continued to grow year after year.[29] The debt service as a percentage of revenue, however, continued to remain lower for the Company than for the other competing powers in India at that time. In the decade of the Third Anglo-Maratha War (1817–1818), for example, debt service as a percentage of revenue for the Company fell from nearer 20 per cent to 12 per cent,[30] even as this rose for the competing powers. In terms of the British expansion in India, debt servicing was not a problem because the opium revenue more than covered it.[31] Indeed, as has been said – not without justification – that as a result of the opium trade, China got the opium, British the silver and India the Raj.[32] And to the extent that India's trade surplus with China was important for balancing India's trade deficit with Britain and to the extent that this was important for the evolution of the world economy in the nineteenth century – we shall see later that this indeed was the case – then the opium trade would appear to have been at the very centre of the evolution of the world economy in the nineteenth century.

India as a source of labour for other tropical colonies

Emigration from India to any large extent started in the 1830s. The first group of Indian indentured labourers was sent to Mauritius in 1834, the year when slavery was abolished in British colonies. Indian indentured labourers were soon after introduced to Jamaica, British Guiana, Trinidad, Granada, St. Luicia, Natal and Fiji. Indian indentured labourers also worked in plantations in Ceylon and the Straits Settlements, and more were brought to East Africa from 1896 to construct and maintain the Uganda Railway. Less formally, many others migrated to Ceylon and Burma: in Ceylon to coffee and tea plantations, in Burma to rice plantations. Overwhelmingly, large numbers went as labourers, but some also went as traders, clerks, etc. Most worked on British-controlled plantations under British managers and supervisions.

An estimate of Indian overseas labour emigration over the period 1834–1924 has been provided by Northrup (1995), who puts the number at 6.5 million (indentured at 1.4 million and those free of indenture at 5.1 million). The effects of this Indian emigration on the Indian economy are likely to have been negligible. India's population in the mid-nineteenth century was about 250 million. The number of emigrants as a proportion of the total population was quite small. The six and a half million or so of Indian emigrants can be compared with the British overseas emigration of the nineteenth century: between 1815 and 1914 about 22.6 million individuals left the British Isles. British population (at 14.1 million in 1820 and 26 million in 1870) was, of course, considerably smaller than India's. Also, the fruits of Indian labour (except their wages) mostly accrued to British businessmen and traders, not to India.

While the impact of the Indian emigration on India was small, the economic effects on the destination countries and Britain were quite considerable. In the West Indies, immigrant labour proved to be an important element in the survival of many West Indian plantations in the years ahead, and "by 1870 the immigrants had helped to sustain a substantial degree of prosperity in these colonies".[33]

So far as emigration to Asian countries was concerned, Indian immigrant labour was vital in helping to make Burma the rice bowl of the Southeast Asia, with greater part of the immigrants to Burma being employed in the rice mills. In Ceylon, Indian labour was equally vital in coffee and tea plantations. Coffee exports from Ceylon to Great Britain increased sevenfold between 1845 and 1870. With disease wiping out much coffee production in 1876, many planters shifted to tea cultivation, and this resulted in equally profitable export trade. Similarly, Indian emigration to the Straits Settlements was critical to its development. Malaya bordered on the shortest sea route between India and China and was to become important strategic and economic assets for the British over time. The Indian labour became indispensable for plantation agriculture in Malaya. Indian labour also constituted an overwhelming number of workers in rubber stations. Furthermore, Indians played a prominent, often dominant, role in almost every phase of development of the modern transport and communication system, particularly the rail, road and telecommunication networks.[34]

What were the effects of all of these developments on the British economy? In judging the overall impact of this Indian emigration on the British economic growth, the following would appear to have been the most significant ones. First, the Indian emigration indirectly enabled Britain to cover a larger part of her trade deficit with the new industrialising countries by her trade surplus with India than would have been the case otherwise: for, as we have already noted, India developed trade surpluses with both Ceylon and the Straits Settlements (with both of whom Britain had deficits) and this enabled India to offset some of her trade deficits with Britain. As we shall see below, Britain's trade surplus with India was important for the maintenance of the British free trade policy and sustained overseas investment by the British, and both of these were important for the growth of Europe and European offshoots. While India's China trade did play the dominant role here, Indian immigrant labour also played a not too inconsiderable role.

The second important point to make is that most of the surplus produced by the Indian emigrant labour accrued mostly to those who would save and invest. Also, there were huge "invisibles" incomes associated with the trade resulting from the output produced by the Indian emigrant labour and these accrued to bankers, insurers, shippers and merchants in London, Glasgow and Liverpool; in other words, again to those who would mostly save and invest.

Finally, of course, increased incomes in the countries where the Indian emigrants went expanded the market for British manufactures and provided employment for many British people, both directly and indirectly.

So the contributions of the Indian emigrant labour to the British economic growth would appear to have been quite considerable. All of these also indirectly helped cementing further the free trade tendencies in the City (more on this below).

Evolution of the world economy in the nineteenth century

The above Indian contributions were clearly of great importance for the British economy at various times and over time. We now turn to discuss what appears to us to have been the two main features of the evolution of the world economy in the nineteenth century, Britain's central role in that evolution, and the Indian foundation of those British policies which were of critical importance for the rise of Europe and the convergence in incomes within the Atlantic economy.

Overseas emigration from Europe and the expansion of international trade

The evolution of the world economy in the nineteenth century was characterised by a very rapid expansion of international trade and mass migration of people from Europe to extra-European destinations. In the nineteenth century population in Europe grew considerably faster than in the rest of the world except for those areas settled by European emigrants. Between 1800 and 1900 the population of Europe and Asiatic Russia increased from about 192 to 423 million (with the percentage distribution of Europeans in the world population increasing from 21.2 to 26.3 per cent, see Table 2.1). The permanent emigration overseas of about 50–60 million Europeans meant that the natural increase of population in Europe, particularly in the second half of the century, was much higher however.

There is no single explanation for the rapid increase in European population in the nineteenth century. The most important reason was probably the decline in the death rate faster than that in fertility. Economic changes then occurring in Europe offered little possibility of absorbing this huge increase in the labour supply, and overseas emigration became vital in releasing this great pressure of numbers.

Table 2.1 Growth and percentage distribution of world population, 1800–1900

	Numbers (millions)		*Percentage distribution*	
	1800	*1900*	*1800*	*1900*
Africa	90	120	9.9	7.5
North America[a]	5	81	0.7	5.0
Latin America	19	63	2.1	3.9
Asia[b]	597	915	65.9	56.9
Europe (including Russia)	192	423	21.2	26.3
Oceania	2	6	0.2	0.4
Total	906	1,608	100.0	100.0

Source: Carr-Saunders (1936).

Notes:

[a] North America = north of the Rio Grande.

[b] Excluding Asiatic Russia.

Prior to the 1860s, overseas emigrants were mainly from the British Isles and Germany. Over the period 1815–1914, the British Isles was the principal source of supply of people, accounting for approximately 37 per cent of the total outflow from Europe, with an estimated 22.6 million people leaving the British Isles during this period. Within the British Isles, it is in Ireland in particular that emigration at crucial stages was critical in providing an escape route from extreme deprivations. Famine overwhelmed Ireland in the years 1845–1847, and in the space of a few years the country lost about a fifth of its population by emigration, starvation or disease. (The population of Ireland in 1788 is estimated to have been 4.4 million; in 1841 it reached 8.2 million and by 1911 it had fallen back to 4.4 million).

As in Ireland, in Germany too emigration was crucial in relieving population pressures at critical stages. Population growth in the second half of the eighteenth century in Germany was already substantial, but this continued to be the case in the early decades of the nineteenth century. There were major crop failures in the 1840s. In the first wave of mass migration between 1845 and 1858, approximately 1.3 million Germans emigrated overseas and between 1864 and 1873 a further million emigrated overseas. Emigration reached its peak in the year 1881: 4.9 per thousand of population.

For the Scandinavian countries, overseas emigration was of even greater importance. Sweden experienced in the late sixties a Malthusian crisis not too dissimilar to what Ireland had faced in the forties and fifties, and 120,000 Swedes emigrated overseas. The next big outflow was in the eighties and amounted to as much as 60 per cent of the natural increase. There were also big outflows from Norway and Denmark. In Norway, between 1865 and 1914, the outflow amounted to over two-thirds of the natural increase. This was a bigger proportion of the total population than in any other country of Europe except for Ireland and, after 1890, Italy.

In Italy, the census of 1871 showed that already by that year there were some 270,000 Italians registered as living in foreign countries – some 155,000 in Europe and 86,000 in Latin America. As population continued to increase and the economy continue to falter, the number of Italian migrants continued to increase from 170,000 per year in 1890s, to 373,000 per year from 1900 to 1909 and an extraordinary 507,000 per year from 1910 to 1914. During the final years before the war, emigration averaged approximately 14.3 per thousand of the population; had it not been for a substantial increase in the number of Italians returning from overseas, Italy's population would actually have declined as a result of emigration.

It is obvious from the discussions above that emigration was of huge importance in relieving acute pressures at critical times in all of these countries. As Thomas (1973, p. 118) wrote, "It is arguable that three outstanding contribution of European labour to the American economy – 1,187,000 Irish and 919,000 Germans between 1847 and 1855, 418,000 Scandinavians and 1,045,000 Germans between 1880 and 1885, and 1,754,000 Italians between 1898 and 1907 – had the character of evacuations". Without the escape route provided by emigration, all of these countries would have found it extremely difficult to grow out of underdevelopment.

It is also important to remember that the structural change that accompanied growth and industrialisation in European countries (many would argue that the structural change was an essential part of growth) would very probably have resulted in major social upheavals in the absence of the opportunity for mass migration. As North (1961a, p. 200) wrote, "The exodus of people under the stresses of the structural changes that accompanied industrialisation and the relocation of economic activity with the expansion of an international economy was an important part of the ability to succeed in such economic shifts without political disorganisation. Certainly international migration contributed to the relatively peaceful character of the century between 1815 and 1914".

As one would expect, European overseas emigration had significant effects on "labour markets at home, raising real wages, improving living standards, and eroding the poverty of those who stayed behind".[35] The effects on the receiving countries too were, of course, quite enormous. In the nineteenth century half of Europe's migrants went to the USA; most of the remainder went to Canada, Australia, New Zealand, South Africa, Argentina, and Brazil. By 1914, the US population, which in 1800 had consisted of about 5 million people, exceeded 100 million. Without any of the costs of rearing and training them, the US labour force was augmented hugely as a result of immigration.

So far as Australia, Canada and New Zealand are concerned, the nineteenth- and twentieth-century migrants mostly accounted for the labour necessary to settle and develop these countries. In Latin America, Argentina was an immigrant country par excellence. By 1914 foreign-born people in Argentina represented 30 per cent of the population – a figure far higher than that for the USA. All these "new" overseas countries depended on the countries of the Western Europe for markets and supplies of capital. They in turn provided markets for manufactured goods. International trade expanded. In 1830 the sum of worldwide exports accounted for 6.2 per cent of global output, this had risen to nearly 11 per cent by 1873 and 14 per cent in 1913, a height not reached again until 1978.[36]

As we shall see below, British invested heavily in these "new" countries. Interactions of British investment, mass migration from Europe and expansion of international trade then allowed many poorer countries in Europe to catch up, in terms of living standards, with the richer countries within the Atlantic economy. Williamson and his collaborators, in particular, have forcefully argued that the convergence amongst these groups of countries between 1850 and 1914 was overwhelmingly due to the open economy forces of trade and mass migration, with closed economy forces such as technological catch-up, human capital accumulation, etc., playing relatively much less important roles. Emigration raised real wages and living standards in countries of outmigration, while immigration, ceteris paribus, lowered real wages in immigrating countries overseas.

Much of the emigration from Europe and expansion of international trade, however, would not have been possible without the involvement of British capital; British overseas investment facilitated and was facilitated by overseas emigration. Additionally, Britain's continued adherence to free trade and the usage and strength of sterling as a de facto international currency were also of critical importance in this context. It is to a discussion of these British policies and actions in the nineteenth-century economic arena that we turn next.

British overseas investment, British Free Trade Policy and the "Sterling" standard regime

Consider first the huge overseas investment undertaken by the British and its consequences. It has been estimated that between 1815 and 1830 British overseas investment amounted to between £76 million and £88 million. By 1854 this had risen to between £196 and £235 million. The real sharp rise began in 1855. The cumulative net total of British overseas investment crossed £1 billion in 1875, £2 billion in 1900, and reached £4 billion in 1914.[37]

As a proportion of gross national product (GNP), the net total of overseas investment on an annual basis had averaged slightly below 2 per cent in the years 1811–1850, but thereafter the rate climbed to stabilise at an annual average of 5.2 per cent of GNP between 1870 and 1913. No country before or since has invested so much of GNP abroad. In 1914 Britain owned 43 per cent of total international investment, leaving France, which was second, far behind with 20 per cent.

Indeed, it is possible to argue that the French foreign investment to any significant extent became possible only after the British adopted free trade (see below). The unfettered access to the British market then enabled the French to increase their exports to a level that generated a current account surplus necessary for foreign investment. Besides, the French invested mainly in other European countries, while the British invested increasingly in overseas territories. Table 2.2 shows the geographical distribution of British overseas investment. The "new countries", i.e., Argentina, the USA and the four white-populated dominions, had the biggest share. It was Latin America which in all received most English capital between 1820 and 1914; but between 1865 and 1914 it was the USA. Overall, India did not receive much. She was an important recipient after the 1857 Rebellion, when the British investment went mainly into railway construction, at a guaranteed 5 per cent interest rate charged against the Indian revenue. Railways were constructed mainly with the military purposes in mind.

Most of the British overseas investment was in the form of passive portfolio investment for the financing of railway construction and other social overhead capital projects, mainly in the form of dock and

Table 2.2 British foreign investment, 1830–1914 (regional distribution)

	1830	*1854*	*1870*	*1914*
	%	%	%	%
Europe	66	55	25	5
USA	9	25	27	21
Latin America	23	15	11	18
British Empire: India			22	9
Dominions	2	5	12	37
Other regions			3	9
Total	100	100	100	100

Sources: Kenwood and Lougheed (1992, Table 4, p. 30); Crouzet (1982, Table 63, p. 366).

harbour facilities. All of these contributed to a massive lowering of the transportation costs and expansion of international trade. Trade expanded especially with the primary producing countries of the world, Britain and then newly industrialising countries exchanging staple manufactures for foodstuffs and raw materials. The "new" countries, as we have already seen, grew with the emigrant labour from Europe. The huge British investment both facilitated and was facilitated by this emigration. Without the British overseas investment and the British market, the volume of this emigration would have been very much lower as also the growth of the areas of expanding settlement.

British overseas investment was also important for the underpinning of the fact that there were no major monetary crises in the long nineteenth century. These years preceded and then coincided with the "high summer" of the international gold standard, a period which witnessed the final triumph of gold as the basic means of settling international indebtedness. Many attributed to this the fact that there were few monetary problems during this period. This, however, would be an oversimplified view.

From the middle of the nineteenth century, if not earlier, what we had was not really gold standard, but what might be more accurately described as the sterling standard. Sterling was the principal medium of international exchange, with gold only being transferred between countries as a balancing item. Sterling was a currency of unshakeable strength and in liberal supply due to the structure of Britain's balance of payments. Theoretically, the fact that Britain had a current account on a continual surplus could have given rise to serious adjustment problems elsewhere in the international economy. This did not occur, however, because of the sustained flow of overseas investment from Britain and because of the country's continued adherence to a policy of free trade. The annual net outflow of funds from Britain more or less matched the current account surplus. Britain, therefore, did not amass large gold reserves with the result that the borrowing countries were relieved of the deflationary adjustments that would have been required under a pure gold standard regime. This again contributed to an expansion of international trade.

British adherence to free trade policy was also very important in this context. In Britain, Corn Laws were abolished in 1846 and the Navigation Laws repealed in 1849. In his budgets of 1853, 1860 and 1861, Gladstone introduced measures which completely freed British foreign trade, and Britain steadfastly adhered to free trade until 1913.[38]

British free trade fulfilled a dual function in the context of the sterling standard regime. In the first place, open access to the British domestic market meant that borrowing countries could service their international debts by exporting to Britain. Secondly, free trade played a key role in the developing network of worldwide multilateral settlement and enabled the USA and industrial Europe to finance their purchase of primary products by exporting manufactures to Britain. Many of the new industrial countries followed industrialisation under protective barriers and it was important that they had unfettered access for their manufactured goods to the largest market in the world; it was also important for these countries that they could trade with and draw on raw materials from the countries where the British had invested. Germany, in particular, would have suffered greatly from an abandonment of the British free trade, for, among other reasons, she had no colonies of any substance. Germany also, as we have seen, greatly benefitted from the fact that the Germans could emigrate in such large numbers to the "new" overseas countries (more on this below).

The Indian foundation of British policies

We have seen above that the British overseas investment, open access to the British market and the usage of sterling as a de facto international currency in combination were of critical importance in shaping the nineteenth-century world economy. We shall now argue that without the British political and economic control of India, the British overseas investment would have been very much lower, the so-called gold standard regime unsustainable and the maintenance of British free trade policy impossible or extremely difficult.

Consider first the case of British overseas investment. To be able to export capital more or less continuously, a country needs to generate a surplus on the current account on a more or less continuous basis. Throughout the nineteenth century, and already during the eighteenth, Britain's visible trade was in deficit (see Table 2.3). As we have already noted, she had a sizeable surplus with India, but overall her trade was in deficit and without this Indian surplus, her deficit, of course, would have been much greater.[39] The visible trade deficit, however, was more than covered by her (large) invisible earnings.

The invisible earnings can be divided into two components: the first is the net income from services, the second is the net income from foreign investment. Consider first the net income from services. Recall that the net income from services (usually known as invisible exports) consists of the earnings resulting from shipping, insurance, banking activities, commissions on re-export trade, tourism, activities/repatriated profits of trading houses and agencies in foreign countries, and transfer of funds by emigrants **minus** the invisible expenses resulting from the government expenditure on diplomatic services, government expenditure on the armed forces stationed abroad (most important of all invisible expenses), expenditure by British tourists, and funds taken away by emigrants.

Table 2.3 Visible deficit and invisible earnings, UK, 1816–1913 (annual averages in millions of £)

Periods for which annual averages are calculated	*Net income from services*	*Net income from foreign investment*	*Commodity trade deficit*	*Balance of payments current account*
1816/1820	15	1.7	−9.0	7.7
1835/1840	19	8.0	−24.0	3.0
1851/1855	24	11.7	−28.0	7.7
1871/1875	87	50.0	−62.0	75.0
1896/1900	101	100.2	−161.0	40.2
1911/1913	153	188.0	−134	207

Sources: Mathias (1969, Table VII, p. 305); Crouzet (1982, Table 64, p. 367).

There can be no doubt that the political control of India was instrumental in generating a very large proportion of the net income from services. There was obviously, first the transfer of funds by the British personnel in India. Second, India's external trade came to be almost exclusively controlled by British merchants. India's exports had been rising from the mid-nineteenth century, and India's export values grew fivefold between 1870 and 1914. "British merchants at Indian ports, principally Calcutta, marketed India's exports generally as well as British imports to India. One-tenth of the entire trade of the British Empire passed through India's seaports, more than a third of the total Empire trade outside Britain. The pivotal role of British merchants in India's world trade enabled them virtually to monopolise its shipping, insurance, and international banking activities".[40] Also, India's China trade and the wider "informal empire" generated large incomes from services. These would have been impossible to achieve without the Indian base and the Indian Army. Indian labour emigration to tropical colonies also helped generate large services income.

Equally, invisible expenses would have been much greater without the control of India, for, as we have already noted, the Indian Army, paid for by the Indian taxpayers, was widely used to further British trade and commerce. Also, as already noted (see p. 22 above), expenditure on "Army and ordnance" was the second most important item of British government expenditure (after interest payment on public debt), and if the Indian taxpayers were not paying for the expenses of the India Army (including the British troops stationed in India) and its use for imperial purposes, the British government expenditure on army and ordnance would have to have been much higher. Indian revenue also paid for the expenses of some of the British diplomatic missions abroad.

So without the control of India, net income from services would have been very much lower. Commodity trade deficits, however, would have been very much higher, for an independent India, in all probability, would have protected her cotton industry.

So far as the second component of the invisible earnings – the net income from foreign investment – is concerned, the genesis of this foreign investment, as we have already noted, lay in the transfer of wealth from India in the late eighteenth century, and the subsequent, rapid rise in capital exports can also thus be seen to be dependent crucially on the political control of India. Without the captive Indian market, the use of the Indian Army, and the Indian transfer, the volume of British overseas investment would have been very much lower. It is also worth remembering, as we have already noted, that India also made Britain a more saving and investing country.

Similarly, it is possible to argue that without the control of India, Britain's continued adherence to free trade would have been extremely difficult, if not impossible. Consider why Britain continued to adhere to a policy of free trade. The City and the financial interests, of course, had no interest in protection. They wanted a greater volume of trade, for a greater volume of trade meant a greater volume of invisible earnings. "Britain's financial and industrial lead was so great that opening an area to outside influences by treaty was often sufficient to ensure that British trade and finance, rather than any rivals', would be paramount in that region".[41] The expansion of the British influence and commerce beyond the territorial empire in China and South-East Asia, and in the Middle East and the rest of Africa was highly facilitated by, if not entirely dependent, on the Indian base and the Indian Army. (We have already discussed the case of China and its significance. In the Middle East, Britain became Egypt's main foreign trade partner, particularly in the second half of the nineteenth century, and there were penetrations elsewhere too, including Turkey and Persia).

So far as the manufacturing interest was concerned, the most important industry – the cotton manufacturing – felt no need for protection so long as the Indian market remained open to them, and new markets could be opened through the imperialism of free trade (with, one may say, the help of the Indian base and the Indian Army).

And agriculture could be allowed to decline in Britain with less political and social turmoil than on the Continent because the manufacturing and the financial sectors were so much more important than agriculture in Britain. (Agricultural sector in Britain had declined to employ only 23 per cent of workers in 1871; in France, the figure was about 50 per cent). Further, the British were able to emigrate in huge numbers to Australia, New Zealand and Canada. "Given the close relationship between Britain and these primary producing countries, British overseas investment in these countries was in a sense almost tantamount to investing in the primary sector of the British economy itself".

Finally, and in a very important sense, India indirectly overcame the foreign tariff barriers for the British economy. While the British manufacturers faced protectionist barriers in the USA and Continental Europe, Indian exports to these countries faced little tariff barriers. Therefore, so long as the Indian market remained open to British manufactures, Indian exports to these countries indirectly overcame foreign tariff barriers for the British economy. As Kenwood and Lougheed (1983, p. 98) put it, "Britain was able to absorb large quantities of foodstuffs, raw materials and manufactures from highly protected countries without having to increase her exports to these countries because of India".

It would thus appear that if Britain did not have the possession of India, Britain's continued adherence to free trade would have been difficult, if not impossible; the total volume of British overseas investment would have been very much lower (if not negligible or non-existent) as would have been the volume of emigration from Europe (and in-migration into European offshoots). The sterling too in these circumstances would have been unable to fulfil the crucial role that it played in maintaining international monetary stability. The volume of international trade would have been considerably lower. Britain was at the centre, indeed the driver of the world economy in most of the nineteenth century, and it was her Indian possession that enabled her to do so. British policies, based on her Indian foundation, contributed to bringing about a convergence in incomes between the richer and poorer European countries on the one hand, and between the "old" and the "new" Europe on the other, while at the same time contributing to bringing about a divergence in incomes between "Europe" and the Rest. Indeed, looked at from a slightly different perspective, the globalisation process of the nineteenth century and its outcomes can be seen to have depended on Britain's Indian foundation (more on this in Chapter 3).

British control of India and aspects of the French, German and American economic development

We have argued above that Britain's political and economic control of India was central to the establishment of an international economic order in the nineteenth century that was profoundly influential for the growth of both the "old" and the "new" Europe. Some of the aspects of Britain's interrelationship with India can also additionally be discussed in some more country-specific ways. We look at some of the relevant aspects of the French, German and American economic development in this context.

French economic development

The French economic development in many ways paralleled that of the English in most of the eighteenth century, and the French were not that far behind the English in terms of economic development.[42]

However, the Revolutionary and Napoleonic wars were to prove highly inimical to France's own economic development.

After the return of peace, France could export by finding a niche where the British were not already dominant. They concentrated on different industries to those of the British, but which often involved finishing British semi-finished goods. They also concentrated on exporting "luxury" or high-quality goods, usually involving a considerable proportion of hand labour, to rich clientele in English-speaking countries. Much of the raw materials for many of these items came from areas of new settlements, such as Argentina and Australia (which, of course, grew with British investment and European immigrant labour).

The other important earner for France became the financial income accruing from the export of capital. However, as we have already noted (p. 35 above), the French foreign investment to any significant extent became possible only after the British adopted free trade. For French capital, the years 1850–1870 were the expansionary period par excellence.[43] Later, when France's traditional exports came up against, particularly American and German protectionist tariffs, it was important for the French economic development that Britain continued as a free trading nation.[44]

German economic development

Opportunities for overseas emigration in large numbers throughout most of the nineteenth century as well as the availability of foreign capital at crucial times (from both Britain and France; with France's overseas investment, as we have noted, being greatly dependent on British policies) and unfettered access to the British markets were all of great importance for the German economic development and industrialisation.

The safety valve of overseas emigration was particularly important for the German economic and political development. As population continued to grow, agriculture was in no position to absorb the increase in the labour supply. Employment in handicrafts continued to grow in Germany even as it sharply declined in France. Nearly 66 per cent of the cotton weavers in Germany in 1875 were still hand-loom weavers and household-based industries in rural areas (such as clock making, wood carving and toy manufacture) had continued to grow as a source of livelihood well into the early 1870s.[45] Certainly, in the absence of mass migration, real wages and living standards for many would have remained repressed in Germany for a very long time. Had it not been for British investment in ports and infrastructure and trade routes lowering transportation costs, German economic development and living standards would have suffered greatly.

Britain also invested in a number of key German industries, such as railroads, textiles and energy supply. The development of the German railroad system between 1834 and 1849 was of particular significance for the German industrialisation. The cheap long-distance transport which the railway provided was essential for making profitable investments in heavy equipment and machinery needed to develop deep mining and establish a large-scale metallurgic industry. Much of the initial development in Ruhr mining and the metal industry took place with the participation of foreign capital (both British and French) and enterprise. Railway building also directly stimulated the iron and engineering industries.

Germany also, as we have noted earlier, would have been hurt most from an abandonment of British free trade policy, the continuation of which policy depended, we have argued, on British political and economic control of India.

Economic development of the USA

So far as the American economic development is concerned, emigration from Europe, capital from Britain, availability of slave labour to do the backbreaking work on southern plantations all played important roles in early American development. In the nineteenth century, it was the demand for raw cotton – as North (1961b) has forcefully argued – which was the most important proximate cause of the expansion of the American economy. After 1815, raw cotton accounted for roughly half of all American export value. British demand for raw cotton to feed its booming mills allowed the American South to specialise in the production of this one export crop. By 1860, as we have already noted, nearly 40 per cent of Britain's exports were cotton textiles. Seventy-five per cent of the cotton that supplied Britain's cotton mills came from the American South. Southern cotton production generated export revenues which were then used by the American East to purchase foreign capital, and thereby to specialise in non-agricultural production. Cotton income also stimulated economic growth in the Northeast through sales of manufactures to the American South. The

Northeast and the South, in their turn, provided a growing market for Western grain and livestock, providing purchasing power to the food exporting West. Without industrialisation and rapid population growth in the Northeast and the South's demand for food, specialised grain farming and livestock production in the West would have progressed less rapidly. In short, cotton helped to tie the country together.

Cotton would thus clearly appear to have played a major role in American economic development in the nineteenth century, and the British demand for American raw cotton would appear to have been very important in this context.

Now it is highly likely that the British demand for American raw cotton would have been much lower and her cotton industry much smaller if she did not have a captive and open market in India for her cotton goods, for an independent India – as we have said previously – would, in all probability, have protected her own cotton textile industry and used her own raw cotton, instead of importing them from America.

British capital would also appear to have played an important role in the transformation of the American economy in the nineteenth century. Although foreign investment financed less than 6 per cent of total investment spending in the USA between 1799 and 1900 – the American domestic savings rate was quite high throughout (most) of the nineteenth century – inflows occurred at critical points and financed projects of crucial importance for the transformation of the economy. Foreign investment played important roles in transportation projects such as canals, turnpikes and regional railroads. In the years 1815 to 1840, foreign investment accounted for 20 per cent of capital formation, between 1869 and 1876 they accounted for 15.5 per cent, and between 1882 and 1893, a little over 10 per cent.[46] Britain was the dominant source of foreign investment in the American economy. And as Goldsmith (1966) wrote, "If the United States had been limited to domestic saving, the growth of wealth would certainly have been slower until near the end of the nineteenth century … because these imports were concentrated in crucial areas of growth, and particularly because without them the development of the American railroad system, probably the main economic achievement of the second half of the nineteenth century, would have slowed down considerably".

The volume of emigration to America was also very large during the nineteenth century as we have already noted. All in all, it would thus appear that in the case of all the three countries considered, Britain's

Indian connections had major and significant economic consequences, in addition to the global effects already considered.

A concluding note

In this chapter we have tried to highlight those features which seem to us to have been mainly responsible for the divergence between the "West" and the Rest in the nineteenth century. The great battle for supremacy in the eighteenth century was to be between France and Great Britain. During the Revolutionary and Napoleonic wars, the British were able to endure the costs of war better than the French. In Britain, the proportion of total tax revenue required to service the national debt had risen from 32 per cent in 1740 to 66 per cent in 1782 (Brewer 1989, p. 117). "After 1763 it was feared that the cost of servicing the debt had outstripped the nation's capacity to raise taxes and that a national bankruptcy might ensue" (Brewer 1989, p. 124). It was this fear which led the government to add to the revenue by taxing the American colonists, with catastrophic consequences. Fortunately for Britain, at about the same time, the transfer of wealth from India became available and Britain was free of external debt to face the Revolutionary and Napoleonic wars. And Britain's position continued to be bolstered by the Indian transfer and other financial returns accruing from the possession of the Bengal revenue (including, as we have seen, customs and tea duties). By contrast, France's position continued to deteriorate owing to the costs of wars. Indeed, it would only be a slight exaggeration (if that) to say that the British success during the Revolutionary and Napoleonic wars rested on Indian transfer and Indian connections. Subsequently, the Royal Navy and the Indian Army would combine to underpin the British power in the world (indeed, as early as 1791, the Indian Army and the Royal Navy together had evicted Napoleon from Egypt). It is India which made Britain the pre-eminent economic and military power, and it is British policies, resting on her Indian foundation, which made the difference between the West and the Rest (and underpinned the globalisation process of the nineteenth century).

Notes

1 The "late nineteenth century" typically refers to the period between 1870 and 1914.

2 See the work of Williamson and his collaborators, in particular, Williamson (1996) and Taylor and Williamson (1997). See also Aghion and Williamson (1999) and the additional references cited there.
3 See, among others, Weber (1905), Tawney (1926), Landes (1998), North and Thomas (1973) and North (1981).
4 See, among others, Williams (1944), Frank (1978), Wallerstein (1974–1980) and Acemoglu et al. (2005).
5 Smith (1776, Book V, Chapter 1, Part iii).
6 See Feinstein (1978) and Imlah (1958). See also Cuenca Esteban (2001).
7 i.e., assuming that the Indian transfer had been zero (my note).
8 India also of course greatly contributed to net gains on trade and services.
9 The opportunity costs of obtaining these imports should, of course, be considered, but it is inconceivable that the benefits did not outweigh these costs by anything other than huge margins.
10 See Bowen (2006).
11 Wong (1998, Table 14.14, pp. 353–354).
12 These are the charges that the colonial India paid for the expenses accrued by British towards maintenance of her colony and were made of three components: (i) interest payable on Indian debt, (ii) interest on the railways (capital investment) and (iii) civil and military charges.
13 See, in particular, Hobsbawm (1968).
14 Kenwood and Lougheed (1983, p. 66).
15 It has been suggested that by 1860, nearly 4 million of Britain's total population of 21 million were dependent on cotton textile manufacturing (see Eugene R. Dattel).
16 See Moore (1999).
17 She also had a large income from interest payments on capital invested abroad, and other invisible earnings from shipping, insurance and banking which went to meet her deficits.
18 See Latham (1978, p. 70).
19 Latham (1978).
20 This section draws greatly on the research of Richards (2002, 2006) and Wong (1998), in particular.
21 India became a major exporter of tea only after the 1850s.
22 Wong (1998, p. 347).
23 Wong (1998, p. 355).
24 Wong (1998, p. 362).
25 The Company had lost its Indian trade monopoly in 1813.
26 Wong (1998, p. 373).
27 Richards (2002, p. 164).
28 Richards (2002, p. 155).
29 Wong (1998, pp. 386–387).
30 See Sykes (1859) and Roy (2013).

31 See Wong (1998, Table 16.2, pp. 387–388).
32 As an aside, it is also tempting to observe that the decline in the death rate in Britain in the late the late eighteenth – to which we have drawn attention in the text above – was gained, to some extent at least, at the expense of the health of a large number of Chinese people who had become addicted to opium.
33 Heuman (1999, p. 485). See also Ward (1999).
34 See Sandhu (1969).
35 See, among others, Taylor and Williamson (1997) and Aghion and Williamson (1999, p. 143).
36 See Ortiz-Ospina et al. (2019).
37 See Crouzet (1982).
38 There was also a movement towards freer trade in Europe in the 1860s. However, this was very short lived and protection rose sharply almost everywhere on the European continent from the 1870s onwards. The USA meanwhile had remained steadfastly protectionist all through. Apart from Britain, Holland and Denmark were the only two other countries which adhered to free trade over the period 1860–1913, but Britain's adherence was the crucial one, for she had the largest markets other countries could send goods to.
39 Britain had a sizeable trade deficit with many countries or regions: the USA (£50 million in 1910) and Continental Europe (£45 million in 1910). On the other hand, Britain had a sizeable surplus with India (£60 million in 1910). It has been estimated that in 1913 alone India financed more than two-thirds of Britain's total deficit.
40 Moore (1999, p. 441).
41 Cain and Hopkins (2001).
42 See, among others, Crouzet (1990).
43 cf. Cameron (1952, 1961) and Caron (1979).
44 cf. Crouzet (1990).
45 cf. Millward and Saul (1977).
46 See Thomas (1954).

References

Acemoglu, D., Johnson, S. and Robinson, J. (2005), "The rise of Europe: Atlantic trade, institutional change, and economic growth", *American Economic Review*, Vol. 95, pp. 546–579.

Aghion, P. and Williamson, J. (1999), *Inequality, Growth, and Globalisation – Theory, History and Policy*, Cambridge: Cambridge University Press.

Allen, R. (2009), *The British Industrial Revolution in Global Perspective*, Cambridge: Cambridge University Press.

Bowen, H. V. (2006), *The Business of Empire: The East India Company and Imperial Britain, 1756–1833*, Cambridge: Cambridge University Press.

Brewer, J. (1989), *The Sinews of Power: War, Money and the English State, 1688–1783*, London: Unwin.

Broadberry, S. (2013), "Accounting for the great divergence", Economic History Working Papers, No. 184/2013, London School of Economics.

Burke, E. in Marshall, P. J. (1981), *India: Madras and Bengal: 1774–1785*, pp. 223–226, Oxford: Clarendon Press.

Cain, P. J. (1999), "Economics and empire: The metropolitan context", Chapter 2, in Porter, A. (ed.), *The Oxford History of the British Empire*, Vol. III, Oxford: Oxford University Press.

Cain, P. J. and Hopkins, A. G. (2001), *British Imperialism: 1688–2000*, 2nd edn. London and New York: Routledge.

Cameron, R. (1952), "French Foreign Investment, 1850–1880", PhD dissertation, University of Chicago.

Cameron, R. (1961), *France and the Economic Development of Europe, 1800–1914*, Princeton, NJ: Princeton University Press.

Caron, F. (1979), *An Economic History of Modern France*, New York: Columbia University Press.

Carr-Saunders, A. M. (1936), *World Population, Past Growth and Present Trends*, New York: Oxford University Press.

Crouzet, F. (1982), *The Victorian Economy*, New York: Columbia University Press.

Crouzet, F. (1990), *British Ascendant: Comparative Studies in Franco-British Economic History*, Cambridge: Cambridge University Press.

Cuenca Esteban, J. (2001), "The British balance of payments, 1772–1820: India transfers and war finance", *Economic History Review*, Vol. LIV, No. 1, pp. 58–86.

Cuenca Esteban, J. (2007), "India's contribution to the British balance of payments, 1757–1812", *Explorations in Economic History*, Vol. 44, pp. 154–176.

Davis, R. (1978), *The Industrial Revolution and British Overseas Trade*, Leicester: Leicester University Press.

Feinstein, C. H. (1978), "Capital formation in Great Britain" in Mathias, P. and Postan, M. M. (eds.), *Cambridge Economic History of Europe*, Vol. 7. Pt. 1, Cambridge: Cambridge University Press.

Frank, A. G. (1978), *Dependent Accumulation and Underdevelopment*, London: Macmillan.

Furber, H. (1948), *John Company at Work: A Study of European Expansion in India in the Late Eighteenth Century*, Cambridge: Cambridge University Press.

Goldsmith, R. W. (1966), *A Study of Saving in the United States*, Princeton, NJ: Princeton University Press.

Habakkuk, J. (1962), *American and British Technology in the Nineteenth Century: The Search for Labour Saving Innovations*, Cambridge: Cambridge University Press.

Habib, I. (1974), "Colonisation of the Indian economy, 1757–1900", *Social Scientist*, Vol. 3, No. 8, pp. 25–33.

Hamilton, C. J. (1919), *The Trade Relations Between England and India: 1600–1896*, Calcutta: Thacker, Spink and Co.

Heuman, G. (1999), "The British West Indies" in Porter, A. (ed.), *The Oxford History of the British Empire*, Vol. III, pp. 470–493, Oxford: Oxford University Press.

Hobsbawm, E. (1968), *Industry and the Empire: An Economic History of Britain Since 1750*, London: Weidenfeld and Nicolson.

Imlah, A. H. (1958), *Economic Elements in the Pax Britannica: Studies in British Foreign Trade in the Nineteenth Century*, Cambridge, MA: Harvard University Press.

Inikori, J. E. (2002), *Africans and the Industrial Revolution in England*, Cambridge: Cambridge University Press.

Kenwood, A. G. and Lougheed, A. L. (1983), *The Growth of the International Economy, 1820–1960*, London: Routledge.

Landes, D. S. (1998), *The Wealth and Poverty of Nations: Why Some Are So Rich and Some So Poor*, New York: W. W. Norton.

Latham, A. J. H. (1978), *The International Economy and the Undeveloped World: 1865–1914*, London: Croom Helm.

Maddison, A. (1971), *Class Structure and Economic Growth: India and Pakistan since the Moghuls*, London: George Allen and Unwin.

Mathias, P. (1969), *The First Industrial Nation: An Economic History of Britain, 1700–1914*, London: Methuen.

Milward, A. S. and Saul, S. B. (1977), *The Development of the Economies of Continental Europe, 1850–1914*, London: George Allen and Unwin.

Mokyr, J. (2003), "Accounting for the industrial revolution" in Johnson, P. and Floud, R. (eds.), *The Cambridge Economic History of Britain*, Cambridge: Cambridge University Press.

Mokyr, J. (2005), "Long-term economic growth and the history of technology" in Aghion, P. and Durlauf, S. N. (eds.), *Handbook of Economic Growth*, Vol. 1B, Amsterdam: Elsevier B.V.

Moore, R. J. (1999), "Imperial India, 1858–1914" in Porter, A. (ed.), *The Oxford History of the British Empire*, Vol. III, Oxford: Oxford University Press.

North, D. C. (1961a), "The United States in the international economy, 1790–1950" in Harris, S. E. (ed.), *American Economic History*, New York: McGraw Hill Book.

North, D. C. (1961b), *The Economic Growth of the United States, 1790–1860*, Englewood Cliffs: Prentice Hall.

North, D. C. (1981), *Structure and Change in Economic History*, New York: W. W. Norton.

North, D. C. and Thomas, R. P. (1973), *The Rise of the Western World: A New Economic History*, Cambridge: Cambridge University Press.

Northrup, D. (1995), *Indentured Labour in the Age of Imperialism, 1834–1922*, Cambridge: Cambridge University Press.

O'Brien, P. (1982), "European economic development: The contribution of the periphery", *The Economic History Review*, Vol. 35, No. 1, pp. 1–18.

Ortiz-Ospina, E., Beltekian, D. and Roser, M. (2019), "Trade and globalisation", published online at https:/ourworldindata.org/trade-and-global ization.

Parthasarathi, P. (2011), *Why Europe Grew Rich and Asia Did Not: Global Economic Divergence, 1600–1850*, Cambridge: Cambridge University Press.

Pomeranz, K. (2000), *The Great Divergence: China, Europe, and the Making of the Modern World Economy*, Princeton, NJ: Princeton University Press.

Richards, J. F. (2002), "The opium industry in British India", *The Indian Economic and Social History Review*, Vol. 39, No. 2&3, pp. 149–180.

Richards, J. F. (2006), "Imperial finance under the East India Company" in Ghosh, D. and Kennedy, D. (eds.), *Decentring Empire: Britain, India and the Transcolonial World*, New Delhi: Orient Longman.

Robinson, R. and Gallagher, J. (1961), *Africa and the Victorians: The Official Mind of Imperialism*, London: Macmillan.

Rosenthal, J.-L. and Wong, R. B. (2011), *Before and Beyond Divergence: The Politics of Economic Change in China and Europe*, Cambridge, MA: Harvard University Press.

Roy, T. (2013), "Rethinking the origins of British India: State formation and military-fiscal undertakings in an eighteenth century world region", *Modern Asian Studies*, Vol. 47, No. 4, pp. 1125–1156.

Sandhu, K. S. (1969), *Indians in Malaya: Immigration and Settlement 1786–1957*, Cambridge: Cambridge University Press.

Saul, R. B. (1960), *Studies in British Overseas Trade*, Liverpool: Liverpool University Press.

Shui, C. H. and Keller, W. (2007), "Markets in China and Europe on the eve of the industrial revolution", *American Economic Review*, Vol. 97, No. 1, pp. 1189–1216.

Siddiqi, A. (1995), "Introduction" in Siddiqi, A. (ed.), *Trade and Finance in Colonial India 1750–1860*, New Delhi: Oxford University Press.

Sinha, N. K. (1956), *The Economic History of Bengal: From Plassey to the Permanent Settlement*, Calcutta: University of Calcutta.

Smith, A. (1776), *An Inquiry into the Nature and Causes of the Wealth of Nations*, London: W. Strahan and T. Cadell.

Sykes, W. H. (1859), "The past, present, and prospective financial conditions of British India", *Journal of the Statistical Society of London*, Vol. 22, No. 4, pp. 455–480.

Tawney, R. H. (1926), *The Protestant Ethic and the Spirit of Capitalism*, London: J. Murray.

Taylor, A. M. and Williamson, J. G. (1997), "Convergence in the age of mass migration", *European Review of Economic History*, Vol. 1, No. 1, pp. 27–63.

Thomas, B. (1954), *Migration and Economic Growth: A Study of Great Britain and the Atlantic Economy*, Cambridge: Cambridge University Press.

Trevelyan, G. M. (1942), *English Social History: A Survey of Six Centuries, Chaucer to Queen Victoria*, New York: Longmans, Green.

Wallerstein, I. M. (1974–1980), *The Modern World-System*, 3 volumes, New York: Academic Press.

Ward, J. R. (1999), "The British West Indies in the Age of Abolition, 1748–1815" in Marshall, P. J. and Low, A. (eds.), *The Oxford History of the British Empire*, Vol. II, pp. 415–439, Oxford: Oxford University Press.

Weber, M. (1905), *The Protestant Ethic and the Spirit of Capitalism*, London: Routledge.

Williams, E. (1944), *Capitalism and Slavery*, Richmond: University of North Carolina Press.

Williamson, J. G. (1996), "Globalization, convergence and history", *The Journal of Economic History*, Vol. 56, No. 2, pp. 277–306.

Wong, J. Y. (1998), *Deadly Dreams: Opium, Imperialism, and the Arrow War (1856–1860) in China, Cambridge Studies in Chinese History, Literature and Institutions*, Cambridge: Cambridge University Press.

3 Technological innovations, globalisation and the emergence of modern economic growth

Introduction

Technological innovations are the key to long-term economic growth. Economists generally regard the total factor productivity (TFP) as being the best proxy available for capturing the effects of technological innovations on economic growth. TFP is the fraction of output that is not the results of the inputs of capital and labour. As is well known, Solow (1957) was the pioneer in growth accounting. His famous study dealt with the period 1909–1949 in the USA when the average annual growth of total GNP was 2.9 per cent per year. His calculations showed that seven-eighths of the growth of the US economy during this period was due to technical progress, i.e., to factors other than the growth in the inputs of capital and labour. Similarly, a recent estimate by Bakker et al. (2018) put the American TFP growth peaking at 2.2 per cent per year in 1960–1973.

By the standard of these estimates, the TFP growth for the British economy during the period of the Industrial Revolution (IR) was very modest indeed. According to the estimates provided by Crafts (2021), the TFP growth averaged less than 0.5 per cent per year between 1770 and 1830 in Britain. Crafts and his collaborators have also provided TFP estimates for the German and the US economies when they were overtaking the British economy in the growth of industrial production in the post-1870 period, and we shall report these findings in due course.

But technological innovations – however one measures their impact on growth – do not take place in a vacuum or fall like manna from heaven. They usually take place in pursuance of profits and when innovators see rewards from innovating. Indeed, they are best viewed

DOI: 10.4324/9781003715368-3

as being a part of the broader social and economic change. One should in particular be wary of any reductionist view that sees the industrialisation of the eighteenth- and nineteenth-century Europe simply as an outcome of technological innovations standing on their own.

There have, of course, been periods of great innovations and significant output growth in various parts of Eurasia at various times in premodern history, but these periods of "efflorescences", as Goldstone (2002) calls them, always petered out. These "efflorescences" were characterised by significant per capita income growth, urbanisation, buoyant regional and international trade, and considerable population growth, but then were "followed by periods of decline or collapse in which population falls or stagnates and living standard declines until post collapse recovery" (Goldstone 2002, p. 342). Examples of "efflorescences" include, among others, the Golden Age of Islam, the Song China in the eleventh and twelfth centuries, the peak of the Qing dynasty in China and the Renaissance in Italy.

Why did "efflorescences" peter out? "Efflorescences" can peter out for a variety of reasons including too rapid a population growth and population density; social complexities and social unrest could undo complex organisational and ecological networks (including cities, roads, irrigation systems, trade networks, centralised governance) leading to depopulation, disorder and "dark ages" (Tainter 1988).

When and why did then innovations stop petering out? As Mokyr (2003) says "perhaps the really important question is not one of why did the great inventions of the 1760s or 1770s take place, but why the wave of technological progress did not peter out after 1815 or so, as it had always done in the past". The explanations offered have usually been in terms of cultural change such as the development of what Goldstone (2002) calls "the engineering culture" in England in the eighteenth century or a change in attitudes and rhetoric towards the bourgeoisie and their activities as according to McCloskey (2010) or "changes in social attitudes to the creation and acquisition of particular kinds of knowledge" as according to Mokyr (2002, 2003). These are interesting hypotheses but are clearly "West centric" and, as far as one can see, divorced from any meaningful global contextualisation. We take a different approach. We have shown in the last chapter the vital role that the British control of India played in bringing about the rise of Europe and underpinning the globalisation process of the nineteenth century. We shall now argue in this chapter that the technological innovations of the nineteenth century were embedded in that globalisation process. Further that it is this globalisation process which ensured that the process of innovations that started with the First IR[1] in Britain in the late eighteenth century – which process itself, as we shall see, was profoundly shaped by global influences – would not peter out this time. Globalisation, we shall argue, was the key.

The last chapter also referred to some of the competing explanations that have been offered in the literature to explain the rise of Europe. Two further such explanations, however, need some brief discussions in this chapter to provide a backdrop to our discussion of the technological innovations in a few countries in the North-western Europe in the eighteenth and nineteenth centuries. These relate to the questions of race and religion. While these variables are not given as much prominence today as they once were, it is nevertheless important to address the question of what role, if any, race or religion may have played in technological and scientific innovations, since the remnants of the beliefs that these were or are important can still be found in the literature and popular discussions (though usually masquerading as something quite different). Section 1 of this chapter, therefore, addresses this question but fails to find any merit in the arguments that they were (or are) important. Section 2 then focuses on what some might consider a related question, but one that is clearly important in its own right, viz., what factors were responsible for the retardation of India and China in the late eighteenth and nineteenth centuries (when the "West" was forging ahead). We conclude that, in the case of India, it was the actions (as well as the non-actions in important spheres) by the British Indian state, and, in the case of China, it was both internal strife and the Western predations that were predominantly responsible for their retardation.

Having cleared the deck, as it were, we then proceed to consider the technological innovations in the West, beginning with the innovations associated with the First IR. Section 3 considers the technological innovations in Britain and finds that in the development of the key industry of the First IR, viz., the mechanisation of cotton textile industry, the global (particularly Indian) influences were supreme and that even in the development of coal-based technologies (including steam power), global influences and the borrowing of key technologies from abroad were important, and that to view these technological developments as being outside of a global context would be a mistake. Section 4 looks at the diffusion of the technologies of the first IR to the continental countries.

Section 5 then notes that the industrial production, labour productivity and TFP growth were all declining in Britain in the post-1870 period and that the impact of the technologies of the first IR was, as it were, running out of steam. There was a distinct possibility of this phase of innovations petering out too like all "efflorescences" in history. This did not happen, however, because a new wave of innovations – some based on the further development of the technologies of the first IR, but many from the development of new technologies – came from the countries in Western Europe (Germany in the main) and the USA, countries that had been benefitting particularly from the globalisation process underway. While the technologies of the First IR were in the mechanisation of cotton textiles production and in coal and steam power, this Second IR was in heavy industries: steel, chemicals, electricity, and also in the development of internal combustion engines and automotive industry.

Section 6 looks more closely at the technologies of the Second IR. Section 7 then considers why was it that it was Germany and the USA which took the lead in the industries of the Second IR. While the labour productivity and TFP growth were declining in Britain in the post-1870 period, they sped up in both the USA and Germany. Section 8 addresses the related question of why most of the innovators associated with the technologies of the Second IR come from only a small group of countries in Europe and the USA. It is noted that there was a great deal of interactions across national boundaries amongst scientists and engineers within this group of countries (which indeed was one of the manifestations of the globalisation process underway).

Section 9 looks at some of the concurrent developments in transport and communications as well as the globalisation of trade in farm output. Section 10 brings all of these discussions together to argue that the globalisation of the nineteenth century was the reason why growth and technological innovations became endogenous to a small group of countries in Western Europe and the USA and innovations stopped petering out. Further that this globalisation rested on Britain's Indian foundation. And that this process led to the great divergence. We also note that the new globalisation of the twentieth century has allowed many developing countries to grow and emerge. The engine of modern economic growth had been set in motion and, as we now know, has since evolved in a way that is now posing serious challenges to some of the erstwhile "core" countries. Section 11 concludes.

Race, religion and innovations

As the Europeans started venturing out from the late fifteenth century onwards and colonised distant lands and shores, an idea of racial superiority began to take hold in many minds, including some very distinguished ones. Thus David Hume (1711–1776) wrote, "I am apt to suspect that the negroes and in general all other species of men (for there are four or five different kinds) to be naturally inferior to the whites". Further, "there never was a civilised nation of any other complexion than white, nor even any individual eminent either in action or speculation. No ingenious manufactures amongst them, no arts, no sciences".[2] Following Hume, Immanuel Kant (1724–1804) asserted that "humanity has its greatest degree of perfection in the white race".[3] Coming closer to our time, Winston Churchill (1874–1965) expressed similar racist views. For example, in 1937 he told the Palestine Royal Commission: "I do not admit for instance, that a great wrong has been done to the Red Indians of America or the black people of Australia. I do not admit that a wrong has been done to these people by the fact that a stronger race, a higher-grade race, a more worldly wise race to put it that way, has come in and taken their place". Churchill has also been quoted as saying that the "Hindus are a foul race" and that "Indians are a beastly people with a beastly religion".[4] For a more temperate expression of the view that Christianity is a superior religion, we can turn to Gottfried Wilhelm Leibniz (1646–1716; mathematician and philosopher; in the Eurocentric view of the world the coinventor of calculus with Newton; they spent a great deal of time quarrelling over who had the priority). In a letter written circa 1675 to a Jesuit missionary in China (quoted by Landes 2006) he had this to say, "What will these peoples say (the Persians, the Chinese), when they see this marvellous machine (mechanical clock) that you have made, which represents the true state of the heavens at any given time? I believe that they will recognise that the mind of man has something of the divine, and that this divinity communicates itself especially to Christians". There are a number of ironies here: first, Christianity, like all other major religions of the world – Hinduism, Islam, Buddhism, Jainism, Zoroastrianism, Sikhism – had originated in Asia; second, the Indian mathematician Bashkara had beaten Leibniz by 500 years in developing calculus (the Eurocentric bias prevents us from recognising this; more on this below); third, mechanical clock was first invented in China around 500 CE, though Europeans rediscovered and perfected it in 1300 having heard of the Chinese machine (see McCloskey 2010, p. 104).

Much has been written, of course, about the impact of religion on economic development and growth. A great deal of this discussion has centred around the Weber-Tawny thesis, which states that the Protestant Reformation created the preconditions for the spirit of capitalism and that this is what led to the emergence of modern economic growth (and presumably continuing technological innovations).[5] However, as has been pointed out by many, some of the most dynamic countries in the early modern period were in fact Catholic countries (Italy, Amsterdam, Belgium) and not Protestant ones. And today, many dynamic countries in East Asia trace their ideological roots to Confucianism, which in many ways is antithetical to the Protestant ethic (see Poulson 1994).

As opposed to these race or religion-based arguments, genetics and archaeology have shown conclusively that people in large groups are much the same all over the world. Or as Morris (2010, p. 16) puts it: "No two people are exactly alike, and each individual is in fact constantly changing physiologically and psychologically throughout his or her entire life; but if we take large groups of people from different parts of the world, the differences average out, and in all important ways the similarities between groups vastly outweigh the differences".

In discussing the developments of science and technology in the West, the contributions of non-Europeans to the foundations of these developments would appear not to have received adequate appreciation, particularly in general discourses, though Needham's (1954, 1964) monumental work on the Chinese contributions are well known to the scholars in the field. Needham noted that in the early seventeenth century, "Francis Bacon had selected three inventions, paper and printing, gunpowder, and the magnetic compass, which has done more, he thought, than any religious conviction, or any astrological influence, or any conqueror's achievement, to completely transform the modern world … . All of them were Chinese".[6] Needham also listed numerous other Chinese inventions, including the co-fusion and oxygenation iron and steel technology.

There are similar studies and findings for India, albeit on a lesser scale than Needham's monumental work: see, for instance, Kuppuram and Kumudamani (1990), Rahman (1984), Frank (1998) and Parthasarathi (2011). India was particularly advanced in technologies relating to shipbuilding, metallurgy and steel-making, and, of course, the production of cotton textiles which found markets worldwide (more on these below).

It is, however, in the development of mathematics – the language of science, if you like – that the Indian contributions stand out. Yates (2017) provides a succinct summary of some of these contributions, and I can do no better than to quote him at some length. He writes, the

> first recorded use of the number zero, recently discovered to be made as early as the third or fourth century, happened in India … . Perhaps most significantly, the decimal system that we still employ worldwide today was first seen in India. … . In the seventh century, the first written evidence of the rules for working with zero were formalised in the Brahmasputha Siddhanta. In his seminal text, the astronomer Brahmagupta introduced rules for solving quadratic equations and for computing square roots … . Brahmagupta also demonstrated rules for working with negative numbers.

'(The) reluctance to adopt negative numbers, and indeed zero, held European mathematics back for many years. Gottfried Wilhelm Leibniz was one of the first Europeans to use zero and the negatives in a systematic way in his development of calculus in the late seventeenth century … . But Indian mathematician Bhaskara had already discovered many of Leibniz's ideas over 500 years earlier.

The historians Bulliet et al. (2023) in their survey of world history put the Indian contributions thus: "The Indian system of place-value notation … and the invention of zero was a profound intellectual achievement. Indeed, it has to be ranked as one of the most important and influential discoveries in human history. This system is used even more widely than the alphabet derived from the Phoenicians and is, in one sense, the only truly global language".[7]

The role of the ancient Indian Bijaganita to the development of modern Algebra has been noted by many scholars (though the Eurocentric bias prevents many from fully appreciating the extent of this). Al Khwarizmi (c780–850) had published a treatise on what he called the "Hindu" arithmetic and astronomy using Indian Algebra in Arabic. An early discussion of the Indian Bijaganita in English can be found in Colebrooke (1817). The so-called Fibonacci numbers and Fibonacci sequences were also discovered in India as early as c450–200 BC, long before the publication of Fibonacci's book *Liber Abaci* (The Book of Calculation) in 1202.[8] As Fibonacci himself acknowledged, he had learnt of these Indian contributions from his travel in the East.

To conclude, much of the foundations on which the modern science and technology are based had been laid by the Chinese and Indians (and indeed by many others) long before the West came onto the fore.

Falling behind of India and China

Given the Chinese and Indian contributions mentioned above, a natural question to ask would appear to be why these countries fell behind in the crucial nineteenth century and the "West" forged ahead. As one would expect, there is a large literature on the decline of India and China and the important contributions include Frank (1998), Landes (2006), Pomeranz (2000), Goldstone (2015, 2021), Parthasarathi (2011), among many others (more is available on the decline of China than of India), and the interested reader is referred to these and other contributions for detailed discussions. Here we focus on the following question: if the great divergence started from the 1750s (or even later), what happened from this time onwards that made India and China to fall behind and the West to forge ahead. We have provided our answer to the second part of this question in the last chapter and concluded that it was the British control of India (and the globalisation process that this gave rise to) that was predominantly responsible for the rise of the West. We now turn to take a brief look at some of the retardative factors in India and China's economic development in the nineteenth century.

India in the nineteenth century

So far as India's retardation is concerned, the primary factor contributing to this retardation in the nineteenth century would appear to have been the policies pursued by the British in India. As Dalrymple (2020) has written: "The economic figures speak for themselves. In 1600, when the East India Company was founded, Britain was generating 1.8 per cent of the world's GDP, while India was producing 22.5 per cent. By the peak of the Raj, those figures had more or less been reversed: India was reduced from the world's leading manufacturing nation to a symbol of famine and deprivation". There can be little doubt that the British policies in India were responsible for the de-industrialisation of India in the nineteenth century. British policies also led to the dissipation of the Indian technical know-how.

We have already referred to the transfer of wealth from India to Britain in the last chapter. The aim of the British in India would also appear to have been to make India a producer of primary products. With the onset of the IR in Britain, the EIC had discouraged the manufacturing industries of India and tried to encourage the development of raw materials. While prohibitive tariffs excluded Indian silk and cotton goods from Britain,[9] British goods, on the other hand, were admitted to India with only a nominal duty. "This was one-way free trade: the virtually free entry of British goods into India and heavy tariffs on Indian exports to Great Britain, direct trade with Europe and other foreign countries being prevented by the existence of the Navigation Acts". The Indian textile, shipbuilding, metalwork, glass and paper industries were throttled, and the internal vacuum was filled by British goods, with India reduced to exporting mainly raw cotton, wool, jute, oil-seeds, dyes and hides to Great Britain. India also, as we saw in the last chapter, started exporting opium in large quantities to China.

The cases of shipbuilding and iron and steel manufacturing provide good examples of how British policies thwarted the development of competing Indian industries. India had a long tradition of building ships. The English private traders and the EIC itself had begun to have their ships made in Indian shipyards, the former from the late seventeenth century and the EIC from the early eighteenth century. By the late eighteenth century, warships for the British admiralty also started to be built in India. Shipping interests in Britain were opposed to this development and mobilised support to have the practice stopped. British Parliament enacted a number of legislations in quick succession. The first came in 1813 with an enactment that barred ships below 350 tons from sailing between the Indian colonies and the United Kingdom. That meant that some 40 per cent of Bengal-built ships could no longer participate in the lucrative India-UK trade. A further Act in 1814 prohibited the Indian-built ships from being regarded as "British-registered vessels" which was a requirement to be able to trade with the USA and Europe. Then came the Registry Act in 1815 which imposed a 15 per cent duty "on goods imported in India-built ships: that only British ships should import goods from south and east of the Cape of Good Hope". Further clauses restricted the use of Indian sailors and mariners. These actions throttled Indian shipbuilding. India's once thriving shipbuilding industry collapsed and by 1850 had more or less ceased to exist.[10]

In the case of iron and steel manufacturing too, the British policy in India was designed to be deliberately obstructive. India had iron-making traditions going back to antiquities, and India's Wootz steel was world famous.[11] But in the nineteenth century India fell well behind as Britain forged ahead with the technology of smelting iron ore with coke fuel and then with the Bessemer process of manufacturing steel (more on this below). Not only was no protection given to the indigenous producers of iron against the British imports (as happened in many European countries), but it became almost a part of the official colonial policy to discourage the development of iron and steel industry in India. As Fraser (1919), an acute observer of early iron and steel industry in India, remarked, the Indian regulations for mining and prospecting "seemed carefully devised to obstruct and prevent development". He drew attention to "the absurdity" of these regulations. "One ridiculous rule was that no prospecting license could be granted to a company or syndicate, although mining enterprises are usually entered upon by associations rather than by individuals … . Again, even a prospector for coal was limited to an area of four square miles, and it was further directed that at least eight miles must intervene between any two prospecting grants to the same person". Prospecting for coal is an elaborate business, involving heavy initial outlay, and such a rule was almost prohibitive. A disgracefully unjust rule was that "when any area has been explored and its value as a field for mining is sufficiently ascertained, provincial Governments were empowered to refuse to grant prospecting licenses, and to put up the whole of the mining rights for sale by auction". In other words, by this last provision, the government, after allowing an individual to carry out all the hard work of exploration, was then empowered to step in and, regardless of the preferential claim established by the explorer's industry and enterprise, sell to any competitor all the mineral wealth that the explorer had revealed! As Fraser put it, "a Chinese mandarin of the old school would hardly have been capable of more shameless injustice". Another ludicrous regulation was that when premises and mines were abandoned, the workings had to be handed over to the government "in a workmanlike state". Even an exhausted coal seam had to be delivered up "in a proper state for working" if the rules were insisted on.

Fraser further noted that these mining rules "were by no means a case apart; they were simply a fair illustration of the normal demeanour of the Government of India towards businessmen". Some of these obstructive regulations were changed only in 1899. In 1903 Jamshedji Tata (1839–1904) started his prospecting operations, and the Tata Iron and Steel Company was formed in 1907. Even then the Company faced discriminatory barriers when it tried to sell its steel to the British market.[12]

In the continent of Europe, as the IR was unfolding in Britain, a number of governments, in trying to imitate and catch up with Britain, had taken a number of steps to promote their industries. One of these was to promote the teaching of science and technology at an academic level with a view to fostering their infant industries. In India, by contrast, as we have just noted, policies were designed to obstruct the development of industries. The state's failure to invest in public goods such as education and setting up of institutions to promote and expand technical knowledge stood in sharp contrast to European policies at that time. An outcome of all of these, as Parthasarathi (2011, p. 125) noted, was that "the highly skilled and knowledgeable workers of the eighteenth century, and the possibilities they held out for economic change in the nineteenth, were dissipated and not capitalised upon". India had de-industrialised.

Decline of China

China's retardation in the nineteenth century can be traced to both domestic factors and Western predations. As the IR was starting in Britain, China was collapsing from a height of economic prosperity to economic decline due mainly to unprecedented population growth and the resultant ecological crisis, compounded by the weakness of the state to deal with the emerging problems, a state that was being increasingly weakened by Western predations and domestic uprisings.

In 1644, the Manchus – then based in the thinly settled northern regions of Manchuria – had seized power in Beijing by ousting the Ming rulers. The Manchus gave themselves the dynasty name "Qing". The Qing conquest brought about major social and economic changes. The most important probably was the replacement of huge bondservant and subservient tenant-farmed estates by a largely free and independent peasantry. "The settling of new territories, the freeing of the peasantry, the expansion of international trade, and the colonisation of new lands in Manchuria and the far West all created opportunities for economic expansion. There followed a period of remarkable expansion, energy, growing wealth, and intellectual ferment".[13]

However, after 1750, as with other pre-modern "efflorescences", this complex structure began to decay. Population in China increased from some 160 million in 1700 to 350 million in 1800 – a gain of nearly 200 million people (Lee and Wang 1999). Ecological constraints began to bind, soil degradation became a major problem in many areas, inter- and intra-regional trade were adversely affected as various regions competed for self-sufficiency, and poorer regions grew fastest in population. In its last century, the Qing was overwhelmed by one crisis after another.

In the late eighteenth century, in response to famine, crowded conditions, and harassment from petty government officials, the leaders of the White Lotus Society in central China launched a rebellion against the Qing.[14] The rebellion began in 1795 and lasted for nine years. Vast sums of money earmarked for the campaign against the rebels were embezzled, and the suppression of the uprisings had long-lasting effects on the imperial treasury. The end of the rebellion in 1804 also brought to an end the myth of military invincibility of the Manchus. It has been suggested that this too may have contributed to the greater frequency of rebellions in the nineteenth century.

By the 1850s the Qing state was severely weakened from several concurrent uprisings across the country. The mid-nineteenth-century uprisings included not only the Taiping Rebellion (1851–1864), to be discussed shortly, but also many others, including the Nien Rebellion. Centred around Huaibei in Northern China, the early Nian Society was made up of groups of peasants who, in dire economic circumstances, took to robbery, kidnapping and extortion.

The Taiping was the greatest of all uprisings leading to what can only be described as a civil war and death of probably 20–30 million people and causing untold damages. The Taiping Rebellion was a millenarian movement led by Hong Xiuquan, a schoolteacher who failed the Qing Scholar examinations and then became a Christian.[15] He established the Taiping Heavenly Kingdom (TPHK) with its capital in Nanjing. During its reign, TPHK controlled much of southern China. The Taiping advance through the Jiangnan region in 1860–1862 devastated what was formerly China's economic and cultural hub. The rebellion was eventually suppressed in November 1864.

Meanwhile, the Opium Wars of the 1840s and 1850s had led to Western nations imposing on the Chinese what became known as the Unequal Treaties. These gave the Western powers substantial control over China's principal ports, dominance of the Chinese Customs

Service (and hence much of the imperial revenue), and extraterritorial rights for Western citizens. China's humiliating defeat by Japan in the Sino-Japanese War of 1894–1895 was followed by still further demands for mining and railroad concessions and seizures of territory by Britain, France, Germany and Russia. However, the partition of China was kept in abeyance as the Europeans could not agree how to do it, nor did they trust each other.

The Western predations and meddling in Chinese affairs eventually led to the so-called Boxer Rebellion (1897–1901)[16] whose objective was the removal of foreign influence over Chinese trade, politics, religion and technology. The Rebellion ended with the defeat of the Boxers by a multinational force consisting of soldiers from eight countries (Austria-Hungary, France, Germany, Italy, Japan, Russia, the United Kingdom and the USA). The Qing dynasty was fatally weakened by the Boxer Rebellion. Following an uprising in 1911, the dynasty came to an end and China became a republic in 1912. And then eventually transitioned to the communist state in 1949.

Thus, while the major European powers were experiencing a hundred years of more or less uninterrupted peace following the Revolutionary and Napoleonic Wars, China was being riven by banditry, a number of major uprisings, a civil war and increasing Western predations. And so far as India was concerned, the country was de-industrialising under the British rule.

Technologies of the First Industrial Revolution: The mechanisation of the cotton textile industry and the development of coal-based technologies

Having briefly noted some of the relevant Indian and Chinese experiences in the eighteenth and nineteenth centuries, we now turn to a discussion of the major technological developments in the West during this period, a period during which Britain had, of course, colonised India. Our focus here is on placing the technological developments in the West during this period in the mix of changes taking place in the world economy at that time. We shall see that it is difficult to think of technological developments during this period without putting them in a global context.

There are two industrial revolutions to be considered. The First IR originated in Britain in the second half of the eighteenth century, based mainly on the mechanised cotton textile industry and coal-based technologies. By 1830 Britain was the only industrial country. However, by 1870 the steam, as it were, was running out of industrialisation process based on these technologies in Britain. A new wave of innovations was needed to carry the industrialisation process further, and the stimulus for the development and growth of these new industries came from the continental countries (mainly Germany) and the USA and resulted in the so-called Second IR (usually periodised to have occurred between 1870 and 1914).[17] We discuss the technologies of the First IR in this section; those of the Second IR will be discussed in due course. In the literature on the technologies of the First IR, the focus has mainly been on the mechanisation of cotton textile production and the development of coal-based technologies. We too focus on these here.

Mechanisation of the cotton textile industry

A number of explanations have been offered in the literature for the mechanisation of cotton textile industry in Britain. We start with the one that sees this mechanisation as an outcome of the desire to imitate the colour, vibrancy and finesse of the Indian cotton textiles and to outcompete the Indian producers in both the domestic and overseas markets. Parthasarathi (2011) has been the most forceful advocate of this view, and this subsection draws heavily on his work.[18]

In the pre-industrial Britain, it was wool – and not cotton – which was the principal textile produced. India was the global leader in producing cotton textiles in the pre-industrial world. Unlike other areas of the world, India had domesticated the cotton plant already in antiquity and by the end of the first millennium had developed a highly vibrant industry.[19] The industry excelled not just in spinning and weaving, but also in the dyeing and decoration of the cloth through the media of printing and painting.

By the eighteenth century Indian cotton textiles had markets all across the world. It was the most important manufactured good in world trade in the seventeenth and eighteenth centuries,[20] and has been referred to it as the first truly global commodity.[21]

Indian cotton textiles began to be shipped to Europe by the various East India companies in the late seventeenth century. In Europe they competed against the major European textiles, linen and wool. To protect their domestic industries, protectionist measures were quickly put in place across Europe: France banned the use of imported calicoes in

1686, Spain and Prussia in 1713. In Britain a partial ban was enacted in 1701, followed by a more comprehensive ban in 1721.

Meanwhile, attempts had started to imitate Indian cotton textiles. These were mainly confined to printing on Indian cotton cloth. In Britain, the printing of calicoes had started in the 1680s. The Act of 1701 exempted white calicoes and muslins from its list of banned items of Indian cotton textiles, which meant that the small British printing industry could continue to work with Indian cotton cloth. And Indian cloth of all sorts could be imported as long as it was re-exported. After 1701, behind protectionist walls cloth printing in Britain took off.

The Act of 1721, however, banned the printing on Indian cotton cloth for sale to the domestic market, though permitting it for export. "This enabled British printers to use white cottons from India to supply chintzes to markets in Europe, Africa and the Americas, but the British cloth printing industry had to find another way to meet the growing demand for calicoes within the British Isles".

This, according to Parthasarathi (2011), led to the search for a domestically manufactured cotton cloth that was suitable for printing. This was achieved by the invention of machinery that could spin high-quality cotton yarns. James Hargreaves' spinning jenny (invented in 1765) greatly lowered the costs of spinning cotton yarn for the weft (in weaving, crosswise yarns are called weft). Arkwright's water frame (invented in 1769) made it possible to produce cotton warp yarn on a large scale (lengthwise yarns are called warp). These were soon supplemented by Samuel Crompton's hybrid machine (invented in 1779 and called the mule), which could spin cotton yarns of a quality that matched the quality of yarns that went into the production of the fine muslins of India. Both cloth printing and the production of cotton textiles for overseas markets took off with the invention of these machines. However, the era of protection was not over. In 1787, for example, an import duty of nearly 100 per cent was levied on Indian muslins, which effectively shut them out of the British market. As Parthasarathi (2011, p. 131) says, "trade policies were integral to the development of the British cotton industry".

So, in the above explanation, it was the search for a domestically manufactured cotton cloth that was suitable for printing that led to technological innovations in the cotton textile industry in Britain, with the state mercantilist policies providing the umbrella under which these innovations could take place.

Turning next to the other explanations that have been offered in the literature to explain the innovations in the cotton textile industry, we have Inikori's (2002) argument that it was the growing demand for cotton cloth in the Atlantic world that led to technological innovations in the cotton textile industry in Britain. Indian cotton textiles were the main medium of exchange for African slaves destined for the Americas (Kobyashi 2018, p. 61). In the eighteenth century, two-thirds of British exports to West Africa consisted of textiles. Between 1720 and 1750, Indian cotton textiles accounted for about half of the textiles shipped from Britain to West Africa. After 1750, the Indian share varied between 30 and 40 per cent.[22]

Inikori (2002) has argued that it was this demand for cotton textiles from West Africa that was responsible for technological innovations in the cotton textile industry in Britain to meet this demand. If indeed this were the primary cause, we would expect to find innovations in both spinning and weaving. However, as we know, innovations were mainly confined to spinning, which would be consistent with Parthasarathi's position that "it was the search for high-quality yarn needed to match the quality of Indian cloth that drove the mechanisation of the cotton textile industry in Britain". In any case, even if we accept Inikori's argument that it was the West African demand that was driving mechanisation, the prior existence of a vibrant Indian cotton textile industry would appear to be of some importance as a background factor as the British were competing against the Indian cotton textiles in the West African market.

A third explanation is due to Allen (2009). Allen has argued that the wage costs were higher, and energy and capital costs lower in Britain than elsewhere and that it is this which led to the development of labour-saving spinning machines in Britain. However, as with Inikori's argument, Allen's argument too cannot explain the concentration of inventive activity in spinning as opposed to weaving. Also, as has been noted by Temin (1966), Tunzelman (2003) and McCloskey (2010), among others, that a major problem with an analysis such as Allen's is that "businesses are only concerned about costs in toto – and not about labour costs or energy costs in particular – so all cost reductions are equally welcome" (McCloskey 2010, pp. 188–189). In any case, Allen would appear to believe that the higher wages in Britain came about because of her colonial involvements, thus establishing a global context.

There is a final explanation which is devoid of any global contextualisation. This is known as the challenge and response model. According to this explanation (see Baines 1835 and Ellison 1886, in particular), Britain's cotton industry faced a shortage of yarn following the diffusion of the flying shuttle which sped up weaving and led to greater demand for yarn. The market forces then led to innovation in spinning, which increased the quantity of yarn.

However, as Parthasarathi (2011) has shown, the eighteenth-century participants in the British cotton industry had a global perspective and saw innovations in cotton spinning as a response to the Indian competition. The challenge and response model arose in the early nineteenth century to be in harmony with the Smithian political economy in ascendancy then. "This led to a re-writing of the history of the British cotton industry in the image of its own theoretical pronouncements, with little resemblance to the actual course of events".

In light of the above discussion, the case for global influences (in one form or another) being at the root of technological innovations in the cotton textile industry in Britain would thus appear to be a strong one. The prior existence of a vibrant cotton textile industry in India producing the only truly "global commodity" at that time, the desire to imitate the vibrancy, colour, and the quality of painting and printing of the Indian cotton textiles, the desire to supplant the Indian cotton textiles in both the domestic and overseas markets, and the state mercantilist policies (including the imposition of tariffs and outright bans) were all important factors behind the technological innovations in the cotton textile industry in Britain. In the case of the cotton textile technology, the technology came embodied in the product itself and needed, as it were, re-calibrating for a different context. It may be noted that the machines of the cotton textile technology – Hargreaves' spinning jenny, Arkwright's water frame and Crompton's mule – were not of a class that necessarily required great conceptual leaps to invent them. The reason why similar sort of developments did not take place in the French cotton textile industry first, for example, surely has to do – to a large extent – with the fact that the French state not only banned cotton consumption, but also cloth printing at critical junctures. Britain's stronger Indian connections were also factors favouring Britain rather than France.

Coal-based technologies

Britain was the largest producer of coal in Europe, accounting for 85 per cent of European coal consumption by 1800.[23] Coal was used not only for heating but also for purposes such as making bricks, glass, ceramics, brewing, etc. Coal was considered to be of great national importance. Government prohibited the export of coal and provided various state support to the coal industry.[24] The development of coal industry over time interacted most consequently with the development of steam power, railways and the iron industry.

Iron industry, like the coal industry, was considered to be of great national importance. Iron products were needed for the army and the navy, for domestic pots and pans, for making nails, for agricultural implements and for various other uses. At the beginning of the eighteenth century, the iron industry in Great Britain was rather small and not able to meet the demand of the domestic users of iron products.

The gap between the demand and supply was met by imports from Sweden and later also from Russia. (Around 1750, more than 65 per cent of the British bar iron supply was imported). Government had earlier levied duties on imported iron to encourage import substitution. Further incentives came from a rise in prices which provided the prospect of increased profit opportunities from successful import substitution.

Iron ores, at that time, needed to be smelted (smelting is the process by which metal is separated from ore by using heat) with charcoal (a wood product) in a blast furnace to produce liquid iron, called pig iron.[25] The pig iron produced by a blast furnace could be poured into moulds and cast. However, this iron was high in carbon – perhaps 3–4 per cent, which made it brittle and unsuitable for forging (i.e., heated and hammered into shape). Most pig iron was therefore converted to wrought iron which could be shaped and forged. The primary method for converting pig iron to wrought iron was known as the fining process. "Fining methods varied in their details, but broadly, pig iron from the blast furnace was placed in a hearth and heated with a charcoal fire stoked by bellows. It would undergo several cycles of melting and reheating, during which the carbon (and most of the other impurities) would be removed. The fined iron would then be heated and worked via a tilt-hammer which knocked out most of the slag, resulting in low-carbon wrought iron".[26] Wrought iron could be used for railway lines, agricultural and domestic implements, arms and armour, etc.

But smelting with charcoal was becoming prohibitively expensive in Britain. The country was running out of wood and charcoal prices rose. As we have noted, the government had imposed tariffs on imported iron. Opportunities were there for import substitution and technological innovations. There was an abundance of coal close to deposits of iron ores, and substitution of coal for charcoal in smelting was an avenue to explore. Many had tried smelting iron ore with coal, but Abraham Darby (1678–1717) was the first to roast the coal (a combustion rock) before smelting.[27] Roasted coal (coke) maintained its heat far longer than charcoal and allowed smiths to create a thinner pig iron.

However, while thin-walled pots could be produced with coke-smelted iron, coke-fired blast furnaces initially were not any cheaper to operate than charcoal-fired furnaces, and "the use of coke resulted in sulphur impurities in the iron, which, while not a problem for castings, made the iron unsuitable for conversion to wrought iron. As of 1750 only 10 per cent of the pig iron produced in Britain was from coke-fired furnaces".[28]

However, over time with the building of larger blast furnaces and the resultant increased heat, the excess sulphur could be removed, thus making the pig iron suitable for conversion to wrought iron. "Coke-smelting took off in Britain in the 1750s, and by 1788 almost 80 per cent of pig iron in Britain was produced in coke-fired furnaces. Outside of Britain, however, where wood shortage was not as severe a problem as in Britain, using coke took much longer to spread. In 1854, nearly half the iron in the US and France was still produced using charcoal. Coke-fired blast furnaces did not appear in Italy until 1899".[29]

However, converting pig iron to wrought iron still required the use of charcoal. Henry Cort (1740–1800) in 1784 "invented"[30] a method of doing this without using charcoal and instead using a coal fired reverberatory furnace on which the iron was separated from the burning coal only by a low wall. The hot air from the furnace was directed over the pig iron to heat it. At the same time, the pig iron would be constantly stirred by ironworkers (called puddlers) with a long rod to release the carbon into the air. The result of this "puddling" process was a highly resilient iron which could be used for making a variety of products – from swords and ploughshares. Cort also invented the heavy rolling process which replaced the less efficient tilt hammer for turning wrought iron into bars. Now iron began to replace timber as the universal working material. Iron could be shaped into sheet iron, pipes, railway lines, etc. By the end of the nineteenth century Great Britain had become the world's largest producer of iron and became a net exporter of iron products. From 1815 to 1830, "exports usually amounted to between one-quarter and one-third of total output" (Hyde 1979). By 1870 as much as 60 per cent of the total pig iron produced was exported. However, and especially after 1850, Britain could only enlarge her export markets by exporting to less developed countries such as Russia and India. The product mix of British iron exports also shifted towards the lower stages of production (from bar iron[31] to pig iron).

We have so far emphasised the importance of coal (and coal product coke) for the development of the iron industry. Besides innovations in the iron industry, the growth of coal mining also additionally interacted with the development of steam engines and railways. The earliest steam engines were the scientific novelties of Hero of Alexandria in the first century CE, such as aeolipile, but not until the seventeenth century were attempts made to harness steam for practical purposes. In Britain, as coal consumption increased, there was a need for finding ways of deepening coal mines. In 1698 Thomas Savery patented a pump with hand-operated valves to raise water from mines by suction produced by condensing steam. In about 1712 Thomas Newcomen developed a more efficient steam engine with a piston separating the condensing steam from the water. In 1765 James Watt greatly improved the Newcomen engine by adding a separate condenser to avoid heating and cooling the cylinder with each stroke. Watt then developed a new engine that rotated a shaft instead of providing the simple up-and-down motion of the pump, and he added many other improvements to produce a much more powerful engine.

The growth of coal mining also led to the development of railways. The practice of pushing small wagons along wooden rails laid underground was common in the metal mines of central Europe, and this practice, it has been said, "may have been transferred to Britain by immigrant miners".[32] From the early seventeenth century, British coal owners began to build these "wagonways" both above and below the surface. Cast iron rails began to replace wooden rails in the 1790s and it was in the coalfields that the first steam locomotive was built. And the steam locomotive on public railways was pioneered in 1825 by the colliery engineer George Stephenson.

So to summarise, the major factors behind the development of coal-based technologies in Britain – beyond the contributions made by the individual innovators – would appear to include the following: a shortage of wood, a rise in the price of charcoal, an abundance of coal and iron ores (deposits of both being situated closely together), the need of the army and the navy, and the mercantilist state support (including tariff protection). Additionally, some building blocks from abroad provided the backdrops: as has been noted, "neither the blast furnace nor the reverberatory furnace, used in coal-field metallurgical processes, were of British origin; nor were the wagonways used in coal mines" (Hariss 1988, pp. 14–18). The steam engine too was not purely a British invention (Hariss 1988, p. 285). It would appear that the British developed them further because they had the most need of them. It is to the diffusion of these technologies to the continental countries that we turn next.

Diffusion of the technologies of the First Industrial Revolution

Continental countries were clearly aware of the changes taking place across the channel, and they wanted to imitate and catch up. The continental governments most wanted British textile machinery and steam engines. However, technology transfer from Britain to the Continent was largely illegal in the early years of industrialisation. To protect its competitive advantage, Britain had banned the export of most industrial machinery (the notable exception being steam engines, which were considered not to be of same strategic importance). Skilled workers too were prohibited from leaving the country until 1824.

The actions of the British government to prevent technology transfer, however, as one would expect, failed. There developed state-supported espionage, smuggling and the illegal recruitment of skilled labour by Britain's neighbours. British machine manufacturers interested in selling as much of their products as possible were only too happy to participate in this form of technology transfer. Smuggling reached such a level that the export bans became meaningless. It was finally in 1841 that businessmen in mechanical engineering persuaded a Parliamentary Commission of the ineffectiveness of these bans. There was also the beginning of appreciation that British trade stood to gain rather than lose from prosperous and developing neighbours.[33]

Belgium was the first country to industrialise on the continent. Like Britain, Belgium too industrialised based on cotton, coal and iron. "In Ghent, English cotton machinery revolutionised local textile production after Lieven Bauwens successfully smuggled the first equipment across the Channel at the end of the eighteenth century. In only a few years, several of Bauwens' colleagues in Ghent had joined the rush to establish cotton-mills. Soon, their red-brick factories dotted Ghent's ancient skyline, and 'Belgium's Manchester' was born".[34]

British coal-related techniques also spread to Belgium earlier than elsewhere on the continent.[35] The natural locational factors of Belgium were similar to those in British iron producing regions with iron ore and coal situated closely together. The 1820s saw the beginning of the construction of coke-fired blast furnaces as well as the use of "puddling" process in the coalmining areas around Liege and Charleroi.

So far as France was concerned, the spinning jenny invented in 1765 was set up at Rouen and Sens in 1771 with financial aid from the French Government and the active assistance of 25 English workmen. Both the water frame invented by Arkwright and Crompton's mule were subsequently brought in, but both of these gained grounds slowly "because they had to be used in mills, which were expensive to build and France at that time suffered from the scarcity of capital and the conservatism of labour".[36] It was through the isolation of France under the Continental Blockade when French spinners were protected from British competition that mechanisation was rapidly adopted. Mechanised cotton industry expanded and expanded most in regions where protection from the British competition was most strongly felt.[37]

While textile technologies transferred relatively quickly to Northwestern Europe, the new coal-based technologies began to be transferred only from the mid-nineteenth century (the exception being Belgium where, as we have just noted, the process had started in the 1820s). It was only with the rising demand for iron in railway construction that ironmasters in large numbers began to switch from charcoal to coke fuel. Behind protective walls, new ironworks in Belgium and France imitated the British model.

So far as Germany was concerned, the French enterprises played prominent roles in the transfer of technology to Germany at this time.[38] Germany in the 1830s was poorly developed with a population that was mostly rural and agrarian. France, by contrast, was a relatively developed nation. French scientific and technical education was of a very much higher standard, and French engineers were in great demand throughout Europe. The German cotton and woollen industries had started with the help of the Alsatian spinning machinery and woollen machines of French invention. But it was in the development of heavy industries in Germany that French enterprises played crucial roles. Germany had an abundance of zinc, lead, copper and silver, but did not have the engineering skills and other resources to develop them fully. France had the need for these metals, and French metal manufacturers and traders invested in German minerals to supply the French market, but in the process, they also transferred technical know-how.

A number of French companies played important roles in establishing the Ruhr iron and steel industry, the most famous being the Societe des Mines et Fonderies du Rhin, Charles Detillieux et Cie (founded in the 1840s). It has been said that it was not until Detillieux's "decisive experiments" employing Ruhr coke exclusively in the production of pig iron suitable for forging from other than blackband ores that the great Ruhr industry was securely launched.[39] And the first German plant especially built (at Meiderich in the Ruhr) for the purpose of producing Bessemer and Siemens-Martin steel – we are anticipating our discussion on the steel industry here (see pp. 71–73 below) – was by the Societe anonyme des Acieries rhenanes (Rheinische Stahlwerke A.G.), a company formed by a group of French and Belgian entrepreneurs, with its headquarters in Paris. "The chief engineer of this company, Gustav Pasteur, was one of the pioneers in introducing the Thomas-Gilchrist process into the German steel industry" (Cameron 1956, p. 304).

French enterprise in the German coal industry too was hugely important. The first modern limited company in the Ruhr coal industry, the Hardenberg Mining Company (S.A. des Mines de Hardenberg), was formed (in 1838) by a group of mine owners and capitalists from Lille, Valenciennes, Anzin and Douai. Subsequently, a number of other French companies entered the industry in the Ruhr and elsewhere in Germany.[40]

Germany, as we know, would go on to become a leader of the Second IR. But given all of the above-mentioned French contributions to the development of heavy industries in Germany, why did France fall behind in industrial development after 1870? As one would expect, a number of explanations have been offered in the literature (see Clough 1946, Landes 1949, among many others), but an important reason would appear to be that France lacked an adequate supply of raw materials needed for the domestic development of heavy industries. As Cameron (1956) put it, "To see the fruits of French enterprise in the heavy industries, it is not in France that one should look, but abroad- and especially in Germany" (pp. 315–316).

But we are running ahead of our story. In the next section we discuss what was happening to the industrial development in Britain in the post-1870 period, before discussing the industries and technologies of the Second IR in the section following.

Slowing down of the impact of the technologies of the First Industrial Revolution in Britain: Evidence from the labour productivity and total factor productivity growth[41]

Even as the continental countries were busy responding to British technological challenges, British industrial growth was slowing down. Imperial impulses were greatly overtaking industrial impulses. Lewis (1949) showed that as far as industrial production was concerned, the 1870s marked the division between two distinct periods in the growth of the British economy in the nineteenth century. Before 1870 industrial production grew at a cumulative annual rate of approximately 3.3 per cent per annum. After 1870 the rate of growth fell to about half that value. Labour productivity and TFP growth also slowed down sharply in the post-1870 period.[42] Crafts (2021) – who has done the most substantial work in this area – finds that TFP growth contributed only about 25–33 per cent of output growth during the period 1770–1860. Labour productivity grew by only 0.46 per cent per year during the period 1780–1800, 0.29 per cent per year during 1800–1830; 1.11 per cent per year during 1830–1856, then reached a peak of 2.06 per cent during 1856–1873, before declining sharply to 1.06 per cent per year during the period 1873–1913.

TFP growth averaged less than 0.5 per cent per year between 1770 and 1830. Here too there was a mid-nineteenth century peak of 1.02 per cent per year between 1856 and 1873, before a major decline. TFP growth averaged only 0.1 per cent per year during the period 1873–1913.[43]

It would thus appear that industrial production, labour productivity and TFP growth were all declining sharply in the post-1870 period. It is also interesting to note in this context that Crafts (2004) found the impact of the steam power on labour productivity growth to have been trivial before 1830. And steam's contribution to labour productivity growth during the period 1830–1850 was only 0.20 per cent per year, rose to 0.41 per cent between 1860 and 1870, and then declined to 0.31 per cent per year between 1870 and 1910. Similarly, steam's contribution to TFP growth was only 0.04 per cent per year during the period 1830–1850, 0.21 per cent per year during 1860–1870, and then declined to 0.16 per cent per year during the period 1870–1910. As Crafts (2004, p. 150) put it, "To base a case for steam power as a basis for the British IR is surely misplaced". (Indeed, cotton textile industry's contribution to TFP growth at 26 per cent during the period 1780–1860 was considerably higher than that of the steam power.)

The picture that emerges is thus one of the limitations of the kind of innovations that were associated with the iconic industries of the first IR. For growth and innovations not to peter out, a second IR based mostly on different technologies and industries was needed. The lead for this, we shall see shortly, came from Germany and the USA. And we shall also see that the labour productivity and TFP growth in both Germany and the USA were speeding up in the post-1870 period even as they were sharply declining in Britain. But before we report those estimates (once again, the important work here has been done by Crafts and his collaborators), we need to discuss the technologies and industries of the Second IR.

Technologies and industries of the Second Industrial Revolution: Steel, chemical, electrical power, and the development of internal combustion engines and automotive industry

Governments throughout Europe in the nineteenth century regarded industrialisation as a process for the state to organise, promote, and control rather than one to be left to the private initiatives alone. Against this background, a number of European countries actively encouraged the teaching science and technology to promote their industrial development. In Germany, in particular, interactions amongst government, educators and successful industrialists led to a significant expansion of technical education and the establishment of technical institutes and university laboratories, and these in turn interacted with the manpower need of the Second IR.

While the First IR saw developments in coal-based technologies and the mechanisation of cotton textile industry, the Second IR technological advances included – besides the widespread use of steel – developments in industrial chemicals, electric power, internal combustion engines (including automobiles) and the increasing use of petroleum as fuel. We turn to discuss each of these in turn.

Technological developments in the steel industry

As the nineteenth century progressed, there grew the increasing need for stronger material than wrought iron. Zollverein in Germany had created the demand for improvements in transport infrastructure, especially railways. America too was expanding westward, and the development of railroads was critical to that expansion. The need was for steel rails. The availability of affordable high-quality steel was also needed for the development of commercial steamships.

Steel has been produced from antiquity. Any iron alloy with less than 2 per cent carbon is generally regarded as steel. Steel has both high strength (in both tension and compression) and high toughness (absorbing a lot of energy before rupturing). It may be useful to set out here how steel used to be made in Western Europe until the 1850s, when a major disjunction occurred. (The production processes in China and India were different and, in some cases, predated by centuries the processes later rediscovered in Europe. But since the industrial revolution in Europe is our focus, we concentrate on the development in the West).

Before the 1850s, making steel was a multistep process. Potter (2023b, p. 2) summarises the process well: "Iron would first be smelted from ore in a blast furnace, resulting in high-carbon pig iron. This pig iron was then placed in a special furnace (initially a finery furnace, later a puddling furnace) to remove the carbon and other impurities, resulting in wrought iron. Wrought iron bars would then be placed into clay chests next to sources of carbon and heated for a period of several days, allowing the iron to gradually absorb carbon, producing 'blister steel'. The methods varied in their specifics across time and place, but this was the general process in western Europe".

The process of producing steel had been improved with Huntsman's crucible process (a process quite similar to the ancient Indian method of using a clay crucible),[44] but that still relied on slow and expensive blister steel as an input. By 1850 steel was still 4 to 5 times more expensive than wrought iron and was largely used in small quantities for specialised applications such as "cutting tools, files, cutlery, surgical instruments and razors".[45] Of the 2.25 million tons of pig iron produced in Britain in 1850, a little over 2 per cent became steel. Similarly, in the USA, of the 560,000 tons of pig iron produced in 1850, less than 2 per cent became steel.

The need for an affordable high-quality steel to be available in large quantities led many people to try to find better ways of producing steel. Success did not come until the 1850s. In 1856, Henry Bessemer (1813–1898), in one of his experiments, decided to pour pig iron into a container rather than let it ooze into a trench. Once inside the container, Bessemer blasted air through perforations on the bottom. The material that was left in the container after the air blow was completed was carbon-free pure iron that – through the addition of carbon-bearing materials such as spiegeleisen (an alloy of iron and manganese) – could easily be turned into high-quality steel.[46] Bessemer built a machine to carry out the procedure: the "Bessemer Converter". The Bessemer converter soon came into widespread use.

However, a problem remained with the phosphorous content of the iron ore. Bessemer in his experiment had, by chance, used some of the only ore in Britain that was low in phosphorous (while most iron ore deposits are rich in phosphorous). Higher phosphorus ores resulted in metal that was brittle and unusable.[47]

The problem of high phosphorous ores would not be solved until 1877 when Sidney Gilchrist Thomas discovered that the Bessemer converter's clay lining was not reactive with phosphorous, so he replaced the clay with a lime-based lining. This did the trick and the new method could now produce five tons of steel in 20 minutes where the old Huntsman crucible process had produced only 60 pounds of steel in two weeks.[48]

Meanwhile, the Siemens-Martin open-hearth regenerative furnace was being developed and would soon compete out the Bessemer process and would dominate steel production for more than 80 years after its first use. German-born scientist and glassmaker William Siemens (who had taken up British citizenship) realised in 1847 that he could increase the amount of time a furnace held its top temperature by recycling the emitted heat. He built a glass furnace with a small network of firebrick tubes. Hot gases from the melting chamber exited through these tubes, then mixed with external air; they were recycled back into the chamber, thus increasing the temperature further.

Siemens' glassmaking furnace, however, took a while before it found its way into metallurgy. In the 1860s, the French engineer Pierre-Emile Martin learned of the design and built a Siemens furnace to smelt iron. The extra heat in the furnace kept the iron liquified for longer than in the Bessemer process. This was an enormous advantage: it allowed ironworkers more time to add the exact amounts of carbon-bearing iron alloys that turned the material to steel. And because of the extra heat, even scrap steel could be melted down and recycled. By the turn of the century, the Siemens-Martin process was in widespread use all over the world.

The Bessemer process had been brought to the USA by Alexander Holley, a railroad engineer, and in the USA, the process was predominantly used to produce railroad rails. "US railroads had begun to experiment with steel rails in the early 1860s and found that a steel rail would last anywhere from twice as long to twenty times as long as a wrought iron rail. By 1883, Bessemer steel rails were cheaper than wrought iron rails, and had completely replaced iron rails in new and replacement track".[49]

However, while the Bessemer process could be used to produce longer lasting railroad rails, in the USA the process had difficulties in producing steel suitable for other applications such as constructing buildings and bridges. Iron ores in the USA did not have sufficient phosphorous content to "make the chemistry go", and the Thomas-Gilchrist process was largely not adopted there.[50] The Bessemer process would eventually be superseded in the USA by the Siemens-Martin open-hearth process.[51]

In the years after the civil war, the American steel industry expanded rapidly. Steel production increased from 1.25 million tons to more than 10 million tons between 1880 and 1900. By 1910, America was producing more than 24 million tons, by far the largest of any country.

In Europe, Germany was the country which most successfully combined the Siemens-Martin and Thomas-Gilchrist processes and acquired a major advantage over its European competitors. While by 1890, the USA had taken the lead in producing pig iron and steel, Germany had surpassed Britain concerning steel in 1893, and pig iron in 1903 (Fremdling 1991). "The annual growth rates in steel output over the period 1870–1913 were 7 per cent for the USA; 1.0 per cent for Britain: 6.0 per cent for Germany". By 1914 Germany produced almost as much steel as England, France, Italy and Russia combined. The lead in steel production had clearly passed to the USA and Germany.

Developments in the chemical industry

Chemicals have been manufactured for thousands of years. However, the development of modern heavy chemical industry (production of chemicals in large quantities for a variety of uses) had its origin in the need to find means of cleaning and bleaching linen and cotton cloth in climate where the amount of sunlight available was a problem. In the early eighteenth century in Europe cloth was bleached by treating it with stale urine or sour milk and exposing it to sunlight for long periods of time, which created a severe bottleneck in production.

Three substances rose to prominence as more efficient means of cleaning and bleaching: sulphuric acid, soda, and chlorine. The manufacturing process of these basic substances continued to evolve over time (Leblanc process being replaced by Solvay process in manufacturing soda, for example).[52]

Until the middle of the nineteenth century, the growing textile industry had used natural dyestuffs. England and France could acquire the required raw materials from their colonies. Germany could not and had to rely on imports from areas outside her control.

The basic product for refining artificial dyes was aniline, which is derived from black coal. Once it was discovered that coal tar contain the aniline that could be used in producing coal-tar dyes, there began a gradual movement away from using natural dyes to artificial dyes. Germany was the country which led the way in setting up aniline factories and developing artificial dyestuffs. The first artificial dye, mauveine, however, was developed by the Englishman William Henry Perkin in 1856. Perkin was trained by the German chemist August Wilhelm Hofmann, who was the Director of the Royal College of Chemistry at the time, and Perkin's work was inspired by Hofmann. Soon afterwards, the Germans developed their supremacy in chemical discovery.

The aniline dye industry in Germany produced many other products besides dyes: these included cosmetics, fertilisers, pesticides, medicines as well as an increasing number of chemical products for the film and photo industries. Many of the products had dual uses (sulphuric acid, e.g., could be used in the production of fertilisers as well as chlorine gas that would be used as a chemical weapon during the First World War).

The big breakthrough in the production of fertiliser had come with the publication of Justin von Liebig's work in 1840.[53] It was he who suggested the addition of chemicals to the soil to restore fertility and thereby launched the fertiliser industry. He showed that bones, after treatment with sulphuric acid, could contribute their phosphorus to plants.

The famous potash deposits of Stassfurt in Germany were discovered accidentally in 1857 while boring for rock salt.[54] Potash output increased from 2,000 tons in 1861 to 11 million tons by 1910.[55] Germany also had an abundance of other natural resources, including ordinary salt, pyrites and coal, all needed for the development of a strong chemical industry. Additionally, Germany took advantage of the latest techniques and equipment. Thus, for example, Germany used the superior Solvay ammonia-soda process (invented in the early 1860s), while the British clung to the outmoded Leblanc process (developed in the eighteenth century).[56]

German progress in chemical industry could be seen by drawing upon some comparative statistics. "Britain's output of 304,000 tons of soda in 1867 and 590,000 tons of sulfuric acid in 1870 was much larger compared to Germany's 33,000 tons of soda and 443,000 tons of sulfuric acid … . (However) by 1910 Germany produced around 500,000 tons of soda, thereby reducing Britain's lead on a per capita basis to about 2.3 to 1. With an output of 1,600,000 tons of sulfuric acid in 1913, Germany surpassed British production by 350,000 tons and even pulled ahead when measured on a per capita basis (1.05 to 1)".[57]

It was in the production of synthetic dyes and new pharmaceuticals, however, that German progress was most impressive. "In the synthetic dye industry, Germany's production of 137,000 tons of highly valued dyes in 1913 gave her about a 19 to 1 lead on a per capita basis when compared to a British output of 5,000 tons. With a world market share of about 85 per cent in synthetic dyes and the largest share in new pharmaceuticals, the German chemical industry had captured a dominant position in organic chemicals".[58] Germany by 1913 possessed the largest chemical industry in the world and was also the largest exporter with a 40.2 per cent global share [see Table 2, p. 6 of Murmann (2002)].

What then explains the Germa dominance in the chemical industry? As we have already noted, Germany had an abundance of potash, salt, pyrites and coal within her borders; the country had developed "the school culture" and had a supportive state. And in Justin Liebig, Germany probably had the most influential teacher of chemistry in the world at that time and under whose influence a bevy of expert chemists grew up in Germany. The Germans also "made it a point to train large numbers of chemical engineers, thoroughly competent in the design and operation of chemical plants. These plants were often in association with engineering and machine shops which made the specialised equipment needed and which could produce apparatus of better or cheaper construction than was obtainable in England".[59] And between 1877 and 1892 alone, the German universities established 17 new chemical laboratories. Germany became the centre of academic education in chemistry. In contrast, "the native Englishman seeking a chemical education before the rise of the civic universities had to resort to a variety of different ways scraping an education. One way was to go to Germany. Virtually all the English professors of chemistry of the later part of the century had undergone this experience".[60]

British industrial development had focused on cotton, coal and iron, and when Germany was developing her industries, Britain was concentrating on being the financier to the world and running an empire. There was the neglect of emerging industries, including chemical (e.g., the numerous uneconomic Leblanc soda plants in the country needed to be replaced with ammonia-soda works. This was not done).

And so far as France was concerned, her natural resources compared unfavourably with those of Germany. The French chemical industry remained arrested until after the First World War. The US chemical industry, by contrast, grew as her economy grew. By 1913, she had become the largest sulphuric acid producer in the world with an output of 2.2 million tons. However, whereas the German chemical industry's growth "was fuelled to a considerable extent by developing new chemical technologies, ... the US until around 1930 developed her own chemical industry largely by importing European chemical technologies and adapting to the American context".[61]

Electrical industry

The development of electricity as a source of power has a long history. A list of the important contributors to this development in the nineteenth century would include, among others, Benjamin Franklin (1706–1790), Alessandro Volta (1745–1827) and Michael Faraday (1791–1867). However, it was not until after the mid-nineteenth century that a number of developments came together to make the electric power and electric motors economically viable.

In the 1860s, efficient generators[62] that make direct current (dc) power[63] began to be produced – most prominently and consequentially – by the German inventor and industrialist Werner Ernst von Siemens (1812–1892) and the Belgian engineer Zenobe Theophile Gramme (1826–1901) in France. (Gramme had emigrated to France at the age of 18.) Siemens had been developing his telegraph systems and was looking for a cheaper substitute for electrochemical batteries. In 1856, he conceived the solid iron armature[64] and called his generator *dynamo.* There however remained the question of how you start a dynamo if you have no power to start with. In 1867 Siemens discovered the self-excitation process[65] which showed how a dynamo (a dc generator) can generate its own magnetic field, enabling it to produce electricity without an external source for field excitation. Siemens enunciated the reversibility principle, i.e., the possibility of one device operating as both a generator and a motor or, what is the same thing, the ability of a dynamo to also operate as a motor (while a generator converts mechanical energy into electrical energy, a motor does the opposite – it converts electrical energy into mechanical energy).

In 1869, Gramme produced the first dynamo capable of generating smooth high currents and voltages. The commercial production of Gramme's dynamo (which was capable of producing as much power as a steam engine) started in 1871. The dynamo was presented at several industrial exhibitions which were flourishing in Europe at that time. The most consequential was the Vienna World Exhibition in 1873. When Gramme was trying to parallel two of his dynamos during the Exhibition, one of them that had its rotor free (rotor is the part of the generator/dynamo that rotates) started spinning while the other was powering the circuit, thus confirming the reversibility principle discovered by Siemens in 1867. All the same, this demonstration had a powerful impact because of the exhibition. "Gramme's experiment also proved that mechanical power supplied to the dynamo and delivered back by the motor could be transmitted along conductors in the form of electricity. This evidence triggered wide interest in the transmission of power by means of electrical lines".[66]

While large-scale generation of electricity had become possible, the question of where to find a large enough market for its uses remained. Such a market was not obvious in Britain where steam power, coal and coal gas dominated the landscape. Continental Europe and North America offered better opportunities. In the USA, Thomas Edison (1847–1931)'s development of the carbon-filament lamp was a major innovation. The commercial distribution of such electric light started with the Edison's American company setting up a centralised power station to supply power to users in Pearl Street in Manhattan, New York in September 1882. Edison used direct current. The system was competitive with gas lighting. Edison subsequently formed subsidiaries in several countries to export his dc distribution system for electric lighting.

However, there was the alternative ac system – electron flow in both directions in ac power – being developed by the French engineer

Lucien Gaulard (1850–1888) and British engineer John Dixon Gibbs (1834–1912) and the ac system proved to be more efficient in transmission of electric energy over long distance as compared to dc systems.[67] The first commercial ac system was completed in Buffalo, NY, during the fall of 1886 by the newly established Westinghouse Electric. There then ensued what came to be known as the war of currents, with Edison championing the dc system and Westinghouse (1846–1914) championing the ac system. For a discussion of these events, see David and Bunn (1988).

However, for it to be commercially successful, electricity needed other uses besides that for lighting (the use of which was confined to the hours of darkness). Electric traction was to prove particularly important in this regard. The German firm Siemens and Halske, managed by Werner Siemens, had presented a demonstrative tramway at the 1879 Berlin Industrial Exposition. It was later presented at a number of other exhibitions in Europe. And in May 1881 the company opened the first regular public tram service in Lichterfelde, near Berlin. Siemens also demonstrated the first tramway fed from an overhead line by means of a trolley pole in 1882. In a few years, other dc electric trams appeared: in Brighton (United Kingdom) and Vienna (Austria) in 1883 and then in Frankfurt (Germany), Paris (France) and Switzerland. The first large public electric tramway in the USA was designed and put into service in Richmond, Virginia, by Frank Julian Sprague (1857–1934) in 1888.[68] Horse carriages soon went out of business in many large cities in both Europe and America. Underground transport system too was transformed. In 1890, the City and South London Line of the London Underground went completely underground and was electrified. Electricity quickly became the norm for powering underground trains.

Gradually, dynamos and dc motors replaced steam engines and mechanical power distribution in factories. "The German electrical equipment industry's annual production volume grew almost exponentially in these early years: in 1890 the figure was around 45 million marks (including 5.5 million for electric motors and generators); eight years later, the figure had already swelled to almost 230 million marks, 92 per cent of it for heavy-current technology. In the five years after 1895 alone, the number of electric power plants burgeoned from 180 to 774."[69] In the twentieth century, of course, electricity would go on to power most of modern industry, a great deal of transport and home appliances.

The emerging electrical industry had its research and innovation centres in both Germany and the USA. Electrical engineering was introduced as an academic discipline in Germany quite early on and laboratories were set up in technical institutes, mainly to train engineers for the industry. Most of the R&D activities were conducted within the industry itself (see Konig 1996). The American model of training engineers was slightly different from the German model. American technical colleges were expected to "teach basic principles and leave practical training to corporations". American industrial laboratories, above all the General Electric Research Laboratory, were highly influential in finding solutions to specific problems by drawing on "basic" research (see Konig 1996).

So far as the development of the electrical industry in Britain was concerned, the British firms in the sector showed little interest in R&D activities. The three major power manufacturers located in Britain before 1914 were foreign-owned, as were many other firms (Fitzgerald 2017).

The output of British electrical manufacturing firms has been estimated at £22.5 million in 1913, with some £7.5 million of exports. These figures compare unfavourably with the German figures of £60 million of output and £15 million of exports for the same year. Telephone usage likewise lagged: Britain had 1.7 telephones per 100 people by 1914, while the USA had 9.7. Lamp output of 25 million in Britain for 1913 was significantly smaller than the USA at 110 million and Germany at 100 million (Fitzgerald 2017).

Germany and the USA had clearly taken the lead in the electrical industry. Germany also took the lead in the development of the internal combustion engine and the USA in the growth of the automotive industry. We turn next to a discussion of these.

Internal combustion engine and the road to automotive industry

Electricity is not a prime mover. Electrical energy has to be derived from a mechanical generator powered by water, steam, or internal combustion. The internal combustion engine is a prime mover, and it emerged in the mid- to late nineteenth century mainly as a result of the search by engineers for an alternative to steam power in certain circumstances. (The steam engine is an external combustion engine because the fuel is burnt outside the engine). The use of steam power required boilers, and the steam engine was thus not suitable or economical for use in smaller industrial units, most of which in any case did not have enough room for the boilers. The first practical internal combustion engine (using coal gas as fuel) was built by Etienne Lenoir (1822–1900) – Belgian by birth, but who had emigrated to France at the age of 16 – in Paris in 1859/1860. The Lenoir engine operated on a two-stroke principle. The engine, however, was weak in strength, consumed a great deal of fuel and was uneconomical. The internal combustion engine became economical after the German engineer Nicolaus Otto (1832–1891) developed a four-stroke internal combustion engine in 1876. The engine used a mixture of coal fuel and air and was ignited by a spark plug.[70] The Otto engine came to be widely used in industrial establishments.

The Otto engine was built for stationary use. The next step was to build an engine that could be used for transportation. In 1885, another German engineer Karl Benz (1844–1929) developed a gasoline-fuelled automobile, incorporating the Otto engine. Gasoline is the most volatile fraction of petroleum and while bituminous deposits had been known in Southeast Asia from antiquity, the exploitation of deep oil resources of the world really began when Edwin Drake struck oil underground in Pennsylvania in 1859. America was also awash with underground oil from its newly acquired territories in the 1840s. The internal combustion engine took to road with great consequences.

The automotive industry spread most rapidly in the USA, with the vastness as well as the scattered settlements of the country also contributing to this spread. Income distribution was more equal than in Europe; per capita income too was higher, and all of these contributed to a higher demand for automobiles. "Thirty American manufacturers produced 2,500 motor vehicles in 1899, and some 485 companies entered the business in the next decade. In 1908 Henry Ford introduced the Model T and William Durant founded General Motors. In 1913, the US produced some 485,000 of the world total of 606,124 motor vehicles" (From Automobile History).

Another important step in the development of internal combustion engine had come in 1892 when Rudolf Diesel (1858–1913), yet another German engineer, presented an engine – since named after him – which relied on compression ignition rather than a spark plug. Diesel's engine was more fuel-efficient, had a higher torque output,[71] and was ideal for heavy-duty applications. Diesel engines came to be used in industrial machinery, ships and locomotives.

As can be seen, it is the German engineers who dominated innovative activities in developing the internal combustion engine. The German school culture would appear to have been important. So would appear to have been the fact that Germany was not shackled to older technologies associated with the steam. The exact role of "science" (technical thermodynamics in this case) in the development of internal combustion engine, however, remains an open question. Diesel always stated that intuition rather than "science" had been the main source for his innovation. Moreover, as Wenginwroth (2000) in a careful study examining the science-technology interaction during this period wrote, "there are not many cases in engineering where science was unequivocally leading to technological development. In most cases technologists 'typically got there first' in advance of systematic guidance by science".

The German and American lead in the Second Industrial Revolution

The industrial and technological leadership had clearly passed to Germany and the USA. During the Second IR, the USA overtook Britain as the world's leading economy. By 1913, the USA produced one-third of the world's industrial output – more than the total of Britain, France and Germany combined. The USA achieved impressive rates of labour productivity and TFP growth. While labour productivity growth in the UK fell from 2.06 per cent per year in 1856–1873 to 1.1 per cent in 1873–1899 and 0.84 per cent in 1899–1913, the USA recorded 2.11 per cent per year in 1874–1899 and 1.72 per cent in 1899–1913 (Kendrick 1961). The USA also achieved much faster TFP growth: 1.7 per cent per year in 1899–1929 and 2.3 per cent per year in 1929–1941. In contrast, in the UK, as we have already noted, TFP growth averaged less than 0.5 per cent per year between 1770 and 1830. There was a mid-nineteenth century peak of 1.2 per cent per year between 1856 and 1873, before a major decline. TFP growth averaged only 0.1 per cent per year during the period 1873–1913.

From 1871 to 1913, German economic growth too was faster than that of the UK. Over the period 1871 to 1913, the growth of real GDP per person was 1.48 per cent per year in Germany compared with 0.81 per cent per year in the UK (Crafts 2020). Growth of labour productivity in Germany averaged 1.75 per cent per year over the period 1871–1913 compared with 1.06 per cent per year in the UK during

1873–1913. More importantly, while the labour productivity growth declined in the UK in the post-1870 period (from 1.18 per cent per year in 1871–1899 to 0.84 per cent per year in 1899–1913), the labour productivity growth speeded up in Germany (from 0.78 per cent per year in 1851–1871 to 1.68 per cent per year in 1871–1898, and then to 1.89 per cent per year in 1898–1913). TFP contributions to labour productivity growth were also larger in Germany than in the UK with the TFP contributions accounting for a substantial share (64 per cent) of German outperformance over the whole period of 1871 to 1913. German TFP growth was sustained, while in the UK, as we have noted, TFP growth weakened appreciably.

What then explain the German and American lead in the Second IR? We have already alluded to some of these explanations in the text above, but it may be useful to present a synoptic overview here.

The globalisation process provides both opportunities and challenges. How successfully a country can take advantage of these opportunities to innovate and grow clearly depends on the interaction of domestic circumstances and globalising forces. From this perspective, both Germany and the USA were ideally placed to lead the Second IR. In Britain, the gentleman capitalists were in full sway (see Cain and Hopkins 2001). Britain was concentrating on being the financier to the world and running a huge empire. Education system was disproportionately geared towards producing "gentlemen", colonial officials, and soldiers. Britain was also shackled to older industries (cotton, coal, and iron).

France, as we have noted, did not possess the raw materials needed for the development of heavy industries (see Cameron 1956) and had her comparative advantages elsewhere (in luxe and finance).

And both Germany and the USA were expanding in a way that both facilitated and was in turn being facilitated in this expansion by the development of the technologies of the Second IR. In Germany, Zollverein had led to economic unification, and this called forth improvements in the transport network. During 1830–1848, considerable developments occurred in the realm of riverine and road transport. Apart from numerous new roads that were built, canals were dug out of rivers like Rhine, Oder and Elbe to facilitate river transport. But the most consequential was the development of railways. During 1835–1840, there were only 679 km of railway system. In 1850 the railway network spread across 6,000 km. In 1913, on the eve of the First World War, Germany had the largest functioning railway network in Europe (63,700 km). The accelerating demand for rail, wagon, engine etc. required a progressive increase in the production capacity of German iron, steel and coal industries, which propelled the modernisation of these sectors.

The political unification of Germany (achieved in 1871) also helped. The annexation of Alsace-Lorraine (a small region on the French-German border) meant that Germany acquired a region whose textile industry was far more advanced than those of other regions in Germany. The technology and skills of Alsace's textile industry soon diffused to firms in other regions, and the German textile industry as a whole quickly grew and mechanised.

Germany had an abundance of natural resources – iron and coal, sodium and potassium – needed for the industries of the Second IR available within her borders. She was also, unlike Britain, not shackled to older, coal-based technologies. It was easier for Germany, for example, to look for alternatives to steam engines and find such an alternative in internal combustion engines than would probably have been possible for a country wedded to the older technology. Similarly, it was easier for Germany to adopt the latest Solvay ammonia-soda process (while Britain remained stuck to the old and inefficient Leblanc process) and to use electricity for street lighting (while coal-based gas lighting continued in Britain).

Germany also had a state and a banking system committed to industrialisation. A "school" culture was nurtured. Technical institutes and research facilities were set up to help the industrialisation process. And investment banks had developed to provide the finance needed for long-term, large-scale investment projects.

Equally importantly, external environment was favourable for growth. Germans could, in times of stress, emigrate in large numbers (particularly to the USA) and maintain social cohesion. Germany had a worldwide market available to her. She had a market not only in Europe but also in areas which Britain had colonised and/or in areas where Britain had invested. British free trade policy was of great benefits to the German economic development. Germany was both benefitting from and contributing to the globalisation process underway.

In sum, Germany had developed human capital of a type that was particularly suited for the development of the industries of the Second IR; she had the raw materials needed for the industries of the Second IR within her borders; she had a state and banking system committed to industrial development; she was not shackled to older technologies; she had a safety valve in the form of emigration in times of stress and structural change of the economy and society; and she had tariff-free access to the British market even as she imposed tariffs on British goods.

Turning to the USA, while slavery was the rock on which a modern economy was built in the USA,[72] the annexation of Texas (1845) and the Treaty of Guadalupe-Hidalgo (1848) (which cemented Mexican cession of the Southwest to the USA) were also important factors in the expansion of the USA.

The federal government actively participated in the growth of the country by promoting industrial and agricultural development. High tariffs were enacted to protect American industry from foreign competition, land was granted to railroad companies to encourage construction, and the army was employed to forcibly remove Indians from Western land desired by farmers and mining companies. There was a growing supply of labour immigrating from Europe, and the country was awash in an abundance of natural resources from its newly acquired territories.

Innovations in steel industry both facilitated and were facilitated by railroad development. The USA was also an ideal country for developing an electrical industry and an automotive industry. In a country as vast as that the USA had become, piped gas could not be transported to remote areas. Electricity was the answer. Similarly, the development of the automobile industry was facilitated by the vastness of the country and the discovery of underground petroleum deposits.

Why did the innovators associated with the Second Industrial Revolution come from only a small group of countries in Europe and the USA

We have discussed above some of the reasons behind the German and American lead in the Second IR. It is, however, important that our focus on the leaders Germany and the USA should not lead us to ignore the contributions of some of the engineers and scientists from some of the other European countries to technological innovations during this period. We have already referred to some of them. But the question may be asked as to why most of these innovators came from only a small group of countries in Europe and the USA. It may be of some interest to attempt to answer this question here.

We have already seen how the technologies of the First IR diffused to continental countries. Latest technological knowledge circulated relatively easily amongst the scientists and engineers within this group of countries. There had been the spread of technical education (including learning by doing); there were the industrial fairs taking place in a number of prominent cities across these countries (and the USA) where the latest technologies were being showcased; there were many cases of professional collaboration as well as rivalries across national boundaries amongst scientists and engineers within this group of countries; and there were important family connections in some cases, the case of the Siemens family – whose contributions to the technologies of steel-making and development of electrical industry were hugely significant – being the most prominent example. The family had three branches and businesses in three different countries (Germany, Britain and Russia), all maintaining close relationship with one another but giving primacy to the German branch when it came to their business decisions. In these circumstances, it was relatively easy for the potential innovators in these countries to identify the particular technological problems that needed to be solved at any given time, and given the state support available in these countries and the presence of markets that were expanding, they also had the incentive to address these problems.

It may be of some interest to elaborate on some of the relevant linkages here. Consider first the case of the chemical industry. In the field of chemistry in the nineteenth century, as we have already noted, Justin von Liebig (1803–1873) of Germany was probably the most influential teacher, influencing chemists in a number of countries. Liebig himself – after finishing his university studies in Germany spent two years in Paris (on a government scholarship awarded by the Hessian government) – working with the French chemist Joseph Louis Gay-Lussac, who was at the forefront of chemical research at that time. On his return to Germany, Liebig moved to Giessen where he built the first chemical laboratory for experimental teaching and attracted students from both Germany and abroad. Among Liebig's passions were agricultural chemistry and physiology, interests that influenced a number of his American students to subsequently go on to establish agricultural experimental stations and promote agricultural education in the USA.[73] Liebig also visited Britain a number of times and his famous book *Die Organische Chemic in ihres Anwendung auf Agricultur und Physiologie* [*Organic Chemistry in Its Application to*

Agriculture and Physiology] published in 1840 was commissioned by the British Association for the Advancement of Sciences.

Among Liebig's many students who would go on to make major contributions in the field of chemistry included August Wilhelm von Hofmann (1818–1892), who was appointed the Director of the Royal College of Chemistry in London on Liebig's recommendation. The Royal College of Chemistry opened in 1845 and attracted numerous students whose interests lay in making a living from the application of chemistry. It was under Hoffman's guidance that the 18-year-old William Henry Perkin discovered the first aniline dye.

In 1865, after 20 years stay in London, Hoffman returned to Germany. Two years later, Hofmann and other leading German chemists set up the German Chemical Society, modelled closely on the lines of the Chemical Society of London, but giving greater acknowledgement to the role of industry. By this time most of the young Germans who had travelled to England to study under Hofmann and worked in the British dye industry had returned to their homeland.[74] Subsequently, as Germany became the centre of chemical industry and studies in chemistry, British professors of chemistry would go to Germany to study in German universities and laboratories.

Turning next to the linkages in electrical industry (and electrical engineering), the various industrial exhibitions of the time played important roles in propagating and disseminating knowledge. We have already referred to the excitement that followed Gramme's serendipitous demonstration of the reversibility principle at the Vienna World Exhibition in 1873 (see p. 83 above). Eight years later, the Palais de l'industrie of Paris hosted the Exposition Internationale d'Electricite between 15 August 1881 and 15 November 1881. It was the first international exhibition completely devoted to electricity and brought together many of the leading scientists and engineers of the day. Many new devices were displayed, including the electric tramway by Siemens.

We have already noted that Siemens & Halske had presented a demonstrative tramway at the 1879 Berlin Industrial Exposition and that it was later exhibited in a number of other European cities. Such demonstrations also influenced the design of first large public tramway in the USA by Frank Julian Sprague (1857–1934) in 1888. It used an original and efficient dc motor that was conceived by Sprague in 1886. This then promoted many similar electric tramways in other large cities, both in Europe and the USA.

Another important exhibition was the one held in Turin, Italy in 1884, where the French engineer Gaulard built a demonstrative plant that extended between the exposition venue and the Lanzo railway station 34 km away to show both the efficiency and safe transmission of ac power over long distances. This demonstration influenced three Hungarian engineers, Karoly Zipernowsky (1853–1942), Miska Deri (1854–1938) and Otto Titusz Blathy (1860–1939) of Ganz & Co.in Budapest, to improve the generator of Gaulard and Gibbs and set up the ZBD (from their initials) system.[75] In the USA, the potential of ac quickly caught on thanks to railway industrialist George Westinghouse (1846–1914), who initially adopted the European technology, by buying both the Gaulard and Gibbs and the ZBD patents in 1885. In 1886, he established the Westinghouse Electric Company.

At the 1893 Chicago World's Columbian Exposition, Westinghouse presented a fully integrated ac system for lighting and traction. This was in contradistinction to Edison's dc system. And the brilliant Nikola Tesla (1856–1943) – who was born in Croatia, then a part of the Austro-Hungarian Empire – had worked for both of them at different times. In 1888 Westinghouse had bought the patent rights to Tesla's polyphase system of ac dynamos, transformers and motors, and it was Tesla's ac system that Westinghouse employed to light the World's Columbian Exhibition in Chicago in 1893. And there are numerous examples of engineers employed in large companies contributing – both incrementally and substantially – to the development of electrical industry.

So far as the development of electrical industry in Britain was concerned, German influences both at the formative and later stages of its development were significant. German influences can be seen as early as the 1840s in the career of William Siemens (1823–1883). Born Karl Wilhelm Siemens in Prussia, he was a younger brother of the German inventor and industrialist Werner Siemens (and who ran the German company Siemens and Halske). William Siemens settled in Britain in 1843 and took charge of the cable making company of Siemens Brothers (incorporated in 1865), an allied firm of Siemens & Halske. Siemens Brothers laid the first direct electrical cable from Britain to the USA. After this success, William Siemens switched to working in electrical lighting and electric traction.[76] German influences in the development of electrical industry in Britain continued with the German-born Hugo Hirst (formerly called Hirsch) who founded the General Electric Company (GEC), headquartered in London.[77]

According to Fitzgerald (2017), "Hirst's two main important managers – Harry and Max Ralling – were also German-born, and in London Hirst initially operated through its sizeable German business community".

And in the development of steel industry, Siemens of the open-hearth Siemens-Martin process were in fact two Siemens' – brothers Friedrich Siemens (1826–1904) and William Siemens (1823–1883), the latter being the same Siemens of the Siemens Brothers mentioned in the last paragraph. As we have already noted, it took nearly 20 years for Siemens' glassmaking furnace to find its way into metallurgy. In the 1860s the French engineer Pierre-Emil Martin learned of the Siemens' design and built a Siemens furnace to smelt iron.

It may also be of some interest to note here in the context of this discussion about the interactions in the development of steel technology and industry that George Lauder (1837–1924), a cousin of Andrew Carnegie (1835–1919) and a partner at Carnegie Steel, and Charles Schwab (1862–1939), another distinguished engineer and steelmaker – under whose guidance Bethlehem Steel would become the second largest steel producer in the USA, but who was then working at Carnegie Steel – both spent a considerable period of time in 1886 at the Krupp factory (the leading producer of steel in Germany at that time). On his return, Lauder used the knowledge thus acquired to build the major armour plate mill at the Homestead Steel Works.

The picture that emerges is thus one of an environment where ideas about technology circulated easily, tacit knowledge was easy to acquire, and there was a good deal of interactions amongst engineers and scientists across national boundaries, but all of these confined within a small group of countries. Others were virtually cut off from this technological milieu. However, this technological milieu did not exist in a vacuum. It was embedded in the working of the world economy. Indeed, the technological developments of the Second IR, we shall argue below, are best viewed as being embedded in the nineteenth-century globalisation process. But before we get there, we need to take a brief look at some of the other pertinent developments, developments both in technology and the structure of the world economy.

Some further developments and the structural change of the world economy

The world was becoming ever more interconnected as the nineteenth century progressed. We have discussed the movement of people and capital across national boundaries in the last chapter. There were also major advances in the transmission of information as well as transportation. There was the increased supply of and demand for both primary products and manufactured goods on the world market. All of these developments were parts of the same encompassing globalisation process, a process that was being underpinned by the British control of India.

Information is essential for doing business. Advances in the transmission of information in the nineteenth century sped up the process of doing business efficiently and effectively in a number of different ways, most importantly by reducing various transaction costs. When one thinks of developments in information transmission in the nineteenth century, one usually thinks of the arrival of commercial electrical telegraph networks in the 1860s. However, as Kaukiainen (2001) has pointed out in an illuminating paper, there were major improvements in the postal delivery systems and reductions in dispatch times a few decades before the arrival of electric telegraphy. "Between 1820 and 1860, global dispatch times diminished remarkably, on average to about a third of what they had been around 1820". Further, Kaukiainen strongly argued that this decline in dispatch times was not a spin-off from new technology of steamships and steam railways but rather due to an active demand, especially from the merchants (including the EIC) for quicker communications.

In the eighteenth century, letters between Europe and the Far East travelled on the same ships as cargos, "and even across the North Atlantic the speed advantage of the Royal Mail vessels over ordinary cargo ships was quite marginal". This state of things changed substantially during the second quarter of the nineteenth century. "Around 1860, a letter from Bombay reached London in less than four weeks, while a cargo ship still needed 100–130 days to sail the ocean route around the Cape; and from New York, a message could reach the City in half the time that a ship loaded with grain needed to sail to Liverpool or Dublin. Similar examples could be listed in abundance".

The arrival of information before the arrival of goods clearly had many advantages for those engaged in international trade. "It made it possible to plan ahead, to sell the commodities before they actually arrived and, subsequently, to direct the ship to the final port of discharge, thus avoiding unnecessary port dues, storage and interest on capital". Improving information also decreased risks and increased the efficiency of market arbitrage. The arrival of commercial electrical telegraphy in the 1860s further improved the situation. It became possible to find out the state of the market for anything, anywhere in the world, quickly and accurately. Business decisions could now be made with more detailed and up-to-date information.[78]

So far as the development in transportations was concerned, improvements in steel manufacturing had major effects on this development. As rust-resistant steel became less expensive, more could be used to manufacture rail lines, making them heavier, stronger, and able to support heavier locomotives pulling heavier loads. Railroads expanded across various parts of the world, linking hinterlands to ports and commercial hubs, and carrying more goods and passengers.

The availability of high-quality steel was also important for the development of commercial steamships. While the first continuous steam crossing of the Atlantic was achieved in 1838, the era of commercial steamships began in the 1850s after coal consumption on ships was significantly reduced. The heyday of steamships, however, arrived only in the late nineteenth century (Harley 1988) with the availability of cheap, high-quality steel which reduced hull weights. Harley's index of British ocean freight rates, which was relatively constant between 1740 and 1840, dropped by about 70 per cent between 1840 and 1910 (Harley 1988). This dramatic decline was mirrored on sea routes worldwide (Findlay and O'Rourke 2007; Mohammed and Williamson 2004). Additionally, the increasing speed of ocean transport also helped cut cost by delivering goods, especially perishable products, faster.

Refrigeration too was developed in response to potential profits on offer by the meat surpluses of the southern hemisphere. In 1861, Thomas Mort (1816–1878) established at Darling Harbour in Sydney the world's first freezing works. This led to further research and development in Britain, Australia and elsewhere. In 1877 the mechanically refrigerated French vessel *Frigorifique* arrived back in Rouen with meat from Buenos Aires, and in 1878 another French vessel *Paraguay* landed a second cargo of meat from Buenos Aires to Le Havre. In 1879 the British vessel *Circassia* made the first North Atlantic voyage by a mechanically refrigerated vessel, and in 1882 the British sailing ship *Dunedin* brought a cargo of frozen meat from New Zealand. This was the start of commercially viable transport of frozen meat, opening up markets in the northern hemisphere to the agricultural economies in the southern hemisphere. The trade in frozen meat and dairy products came to be dominated by British firms.

Agricultural globalisation was taking place as a part of the nineteenth-century globalisation process. IR had delivered farm machinery, chemical fertilisers and pesticides. Farm output increased in a number of countries. Global output of primary products increased as people emigrated from Europe to farm new land in the land-abundant, labour-scarce New World countries, and the Chinese and Indians emigrated mostly to tropical colonies to grow mostly primary products. Intra-national transport and communication costs were also declining due to improvements in rail transport.

The size of the market for agricultural products grew everywhere. Population growth, increased per capita income in a number of countries, improved infrastructure facilities all interacted with market growth. There were also shifts away from subsistence strategies by many farmers, shifts that were often promoted by the state. Trade in agricultural products took off. Settler countries such as Argentina, Peru, Australia and Canada increased their production and supply of output particularly significantly. The only estimates carried out regarding the growth in agricultural production on a global scale highlight that, between 1870 and 1938, growth increased at an average annual rate of 1.3 per cent (Federico 2004). The annual growth rates of settler countries, however, were very much higher (usually above 6 per cent) during the conquest of new territories and the displacement of the frontier westward.

As one would expect, international trade in agricultural goods expanded rapidly. The estimates performed by Lewis (1952, 1981) for primary products as a whole indicate an annual growth rate of 3.7 per cent between 1850 and 1900. According to Federico (2005), world exports of both agricultural and non-agricultural goods grew on average at almost 3.5 per cent per year between 1850 and 1913, well ahead of the annual rate of global farm output growth of 1.1 per cent between 1870 and 1913. During this period trade was certainly interindustry, i.e., the predominant tendency was the exchange of raw materials and food products for manufactured goods.

A new international trading order came into existence where the "core" exported manufactured goods, the "periphery" primary products. In the New World system that developed, areas of new settlements and other "peripheries" provided primary products and raw materials, new industrial countries provided modern manufactured goods while Britain provided "old" manufactured goods, but most importantly she provided financial services to all comers. The continental European nations, as a group, balanced imports of temperate and tropical foodstuffs and raw materials primarily by exporting manufactured goods to Britain. Britain, in turn, earned surpluses by selling manufactured goods to the periphery (mostly to India), from returns on shipping and financial services and from large overseas investment. I have in the last chapter discussed the vital role that the British control of India played in underpinning the whole of this system.

Globalisation and innovations or why growth and innovations stopped petering out

We are now in a position to provide our answer to the question as to why the process of technological innovations that started with the First IR did not peter out (as various "efflorescences" had done in history). The answer at one level is, of course, quite a straightforward one and the one that we have already discussed. Technological innovations did not peter out because the Second IR took place. The important point, however, is that these developments occurred as a part and parcel of a world that was globalising and globalising in a way very different from the previous globalisations in history.

For growth to have become modern and sustainable, growth needed to spread to at least a few other countries outside of Britain, and that growth needed to be sustained. The nineteenth-century globalisation process ensured this. Technological innovations were embedded in the nineteenth-century globalisation process. The various elements that made up this globalisation in combination provided the mechanism for modern growth to emerge within a small group of countries in Western Europe (and the USA) and for technological innovations and their diffusions to be a continuing process within this group. Technological innovations did not peter out within this group of countries because growth did not peter out, and growth did not peter out because technological innovations did not peter out. And the two did not peter out because a new kind of globalisation had taken place.

The globalisation of the nineteenth century was fundamentally different from previous globalisations in history. Previous globalisations had been predominantly globalisation of trade. The nineteenth century globalisation was much more than the globalisation of trade, though a huge expansion of inter-continental and intra-continental trade was also a part of this globalisation process (the ratio of world trade to world GDP increased from somewhere between 2 and 8 per cent around 1800 to roughly 20 per cent by the end of the nineteenth century (Estevadeordal et al. 2003, p. 360)). It may be useful here to recall some of the other key elements of the nineteenth century globalisation process. These included:

- an historically unprecedented volume of foreign investment, mainly in infrastructure development and mainly by Britain; also, considerable investment by France mainly within Europe (including Germany, Italy, Spain and Russia) and the Near East;
- a huge number of people emigrating from Europe to (the land-abundant) Americas and "areas of settlements"; also, a large volume of emigration of Indian and Chinese labourers, mostly to the tropical colonies;
- the continuing impact of slave labour in the plantations of Americas;
- the establishment, as it were, of an agricultural sector overseas (for Britain in particular) and the globalisation of trade in agricultural output, accompanied by a huge expansion of trade in primary products for manufactured goods;
- the ease of diffusion of technology amongst a subset of countries in Europe (and the USA) via contacts, imitations, smuggling and emigration; Germany, in particular. benefitted from the French tutelage;
- an overarching global financial system based on the City of London;
- the gradual use of sterling as a de fact international currency;
- and all of these elements interacting with one another and with a generally peaceful nature of the world for major European powers between 1815 and 1913.

All of the above elements came together to ensure that growth and innovations would not peter out in the "core" group of countries this time around. Indeed, it may be useful here to list some of the specific ways in which a globalisation process of the nineteenth century-type can lead to continuing technological innovations within a subset of countries. The list below is by no means exhaustive. With the unfolding of such a globalisation process:

- the size of the market available to potential innovators and entrepreneurs becomes larger, as do the potential pay-offs;

- the complementary investment needed to bring ideas and innovations to the market becomes more readily available as capital becomes available from wider sources and across national boundaries;[79]
- ideas travel faster both within and across national boundaries, though predominantly within the "core" group of countries;
- the effective transmission of technological knowledge is significantly bolstered via personal contacts, trade fares, scientific conferences, etc. Technological knowledge is often tacit knowledge, rules of performance cannot always be fully spelled out, and effective transmission often requires personal contacts; such contacts are enhanced by the globalisation process;
- the diffusion of novel technological advances made in one country leads to further technological advances elsewhere within the group as some of the adopters try to adapt these technologies to suit their particular needs and circumstances (including their resource base) and build on them. This may then lead to yet further technological advances in the process;[80]
- the accumulation of human capital is greatly bolstered. The increased opportunities available now provide incentives to individuals to accumulate human capital. (The state as well as private provisions of technical education, the establishment of R&D facilities, etc. can also be designed to lead to the accumulation of the desired type of human capital). An increase in the stock of human capital in any country within the "core" group has positive externalities for the other members of the group. There develops a synergism in ideas such that there is a rapid increase in the stock of knowledge over time, thus providing the foundation for further technological advances. (In such a world, any slowing down of technological advances in any one country need not lead to a slowing down of technological advances overall).

The nineteenth century-type globalisation process would thus seem to contain within itself several pathways through which technological innovations could be generated and diffused in a continuing way in the "core" group of countries. It is, however, the case – as we already have had occasions to note before – that the globalisation of the nineteenth century, while based on Britain's Indian foundation, left India, China and most of the "non-European" world behind. India deindustrialised and China fell into deep political and economic malaise. There occurred the great divergence.

The nineteenth-century globalisation came to an end with the outbreak of the First World War in 1914. The Western powers had used their military superiority to build enormous empires. Even as early as the late fifteenth/early sixteenth century their gun-bearing sailing vessel as an engine of war far outclassed anything they met in Asian waters. For various reasons into which we do not need to go here, the West had applied itself to military matters with enormous enthusiasm and success.[81] And as Hacker (1977) has noted, the first half of the nineteenth century saw "the opening stages of a revolutionary transformation of Western military and naval technology. The smoothbore flintlock musket that equipped European armies in 1800, itself a long step beyond the matchlocks still used in the East, had given way by mid-century to the caplock rifled musket. Artillery had become more mobile, and breech-loading rifled ordnance firing explosive shells had begun to replace the older muzzle-loading smoothbores both on land and at sea. Shell guns were but one aspect of a naval revolution whose most important feature, steam propulsion, was already well established by mid-century" (p. 47). During the First World War Europeans turned against each other the killing power they had tested mainly in Africa and Asia during the nineteenth century. The globalisation of the nineteenth century came to an end.

The new wave of globalisation that started after the Second World War has allowed many Asian countries – all independent now and mostly able to take their own independent decisions – to forge their own ways and take advantage of the opportunities available in the global economy to grow, to set up their own R&D and educational facilities. Countries such as Japan, S. Korea, Taiwan and China (China in AI and space technology) are now contributing to the frontier technology. Other countries (including India) can also be expected to contribute to these developments in the future. And certainly, the pool of talents from which new innovation can emerge can but only grow with time.

Conclusion

In this chapter we have emphasised the role of global influences in the development of the technologies of both the First and Second IRs. Technologies of the Second IR, in particular, were deeply embedded in the globalisation process of the nineteenth century – a globalisation process that was underpinned by the British control of India. It is this embeddedness that ensured that growth and innovations would not peter out this time as they had after various "efflorescences" in history. While Germany and the USA were the leaders in the technologies and industries of the Second IR, contributions to technological advancements also came from the innovators and engineers from some of the other European countries who were linked by personal and professional contacts across national boundaries, were well familiar with the urgent technological problems that needed to be solved, and in general had supportive states. These developments interacted with a generally peaceful period of a century or so for the major European powers and the establishment of a global economic order where the "periphery" supplied mostly primary goods and raw materials and the "core" manufactured goods (with Britain providing financial services to all comers). There was at the same time a massive movement of people from Europe to the USA and the "areas of settlements", which provided the labour needed for their development while at the same time easing the pressure of population in Europe.

And while Europe was enjoying a prolonged period of peace, China was being riven by domestic chaos and Western predations, and India was de-industrialising under the British rule. As the West forged ahead, the rest fell behind (these two outcomes in many ways being the two sides of the same coin). But the engine of modern economic growth had been set in motion and on a path that would, as we now know, evolve in a way that would pose serious challenges to some of the erstwhile "core" countries.

Notes

1 The first to distinguish it from the Second IR. See the discussions on pp. 64–65.
2 See Hume (1748).
3 See Kant (1803).
4 See Gerard DeGroot's review of "Fighting Retreat: Churchill and India" by Walter Reid, published by Hurst in 2023; Groot's review is in *The Times*, 6 January 2024.
5 See Weber (1905) and Tawney (1926).
6 Quoted by McCloskey (2010, p. 104).
7 The Indian system spread to the Middle East, Southeast Asia and East Asia by the seventh century, and to the Christian West by the late tenth/early eleventh century.
8 See, among others, Singh (1985),

9 In 1813, for example, the importers of Indian calicoes into Great Britain had to pay a duty of 78 per cent on their imports (otherwise the Indian calicoes would have sold at a price 50–60 per cent lower than that of their English equivalents).

10 The collapse had nothing to do with the development of steam vessels. Bengal had shown great expertise in building steel vessels before the various discriminatory policies made it uneconomical to do so. See Tharoor (2016).

11 See, among others, Srinivasan and Ranganathan (2004).

12 cf. Tharoor (2016, pp. 31–32).

13 Goldstone (2002, p. 348).

14 The White Lotus Society had first appeared in the late thirteenth century in protest against the Mongol rule. The Society's ideology included a belief in the return of the Buddha. Their rebellion against the Mongols – who they considered to be outsiders – eventually came to be led by a Buddhist monk, Zhu Yuen-Zhang, who, after defeating the Mongols, established the Ming dynasty (1368–1644). After the Manchus overthrew the Mings, the members of the White Lotus Society (who regarded the Manchus as foreign usurpers) persisted in wanting to see the return of the Ming dynasty.

15 He claimed to be the second son of God and the younger brother of Jesus Christ (Spence 1996).

16 The Boxers were so named because most of the followers of the movement practised martial arts, including boxing.

17 Like most periodisation, this particular periodisation can also be questioned, particularly with respect to developments in the USA. However, we stick to this widely accepted periodisation here. The substance of our arguments is not affected by this periodisation.

18 See also the works of Riello (2010) and Kobayashi (2018).

19 See Riello (2010).

20 cf. Darwin (2008, p. 193) and Findlay and O'Rourke (2007, p. 355).

21 cf. Riello (2010).

22 Indian cotton textiles also had a predominant position among the commodities carried by ships of other European countries to West and West-Central Africa. Kobayashi (2018) cites Jean Tarrade, the acknowledged expert on early modern French colonial trade, to the effect that in the late eighteenth century Indian cotton goods accounted for 40 per cent of total French exports to Africa.

23 See Malanima (2001, p. 57).

24 cf. Parthasarathi (2011, p. 30).

25 Iron ores could not be smelted with hard coal because the coal's trace elements, especially sulphur, are damaging to the metal. Charcoal had to be used instead. The blast furnace had been in use in China since the fifth century BC. "Workers dug trenches on the foundry floor that branched out

from a long central channel, making space for the liquid iron to flow. The trenches resembled a litter of suckling piglets and thus a nickname was born: pig iron". The blast furnace as it came to England came from "the Liege area of modern Belgium, whence it spread into northern France and then across the Channel to the Weald of Sussex" (Harris 1988, p. 14).

26 Potter (2023a, p. 7).

27 Darby had spent much of his childhood working in malt mills where roasting coal in the process of grinding barley was common.

28 Potter (2023a, p. 9).

29 Potter (2023a, p. 9).

30 I put the word "invented" within inverted commas here advisedly. There has been recent controversy regarding whether Cort invented the wrought iron-making processes he is credited with. Bulstrode (2023) has argued that such processes in fact were actually pioneered by black Jamaican iron mill workers, many of whom were enslaved. However, Bulstrode's paper has been heavily criticised by other scholars who have claimed that the paper "lacks substantive evidence to validate its claims".

31 That is, wrought iron in the form of bars.

32 cf. Macleod (2004, p. 117).

33 cf. Wengenroth (2000).

34 See Hilden (1993, p. 19).

35 Indeed, the knowledge of blast furnace had originally come to Britain from Belgium via France. See Harris (1988, p. 14).

36 See Dunham (1928).

37 See Juhasz (2018).

38 The following discussion is based on Cameron (1956).

39 Benaerts (1933, cited by Cameron 1956).

40 French influences on German financial institutions have, of course, been long recognised. The great German credit banks which played such key roles in German industrialisation in the last half of the nineteenth century had as their inspiration the French Credit Mobilier and the French "universal banking" system. See, among others, Gerschenkron (1962).

41 This section relies heavily on the research conducted by Crafts and his collaborators (see, in particular, Crafts 2004, 2020; Crafts and Woltjer 2021; and Bakker et al. 2018).

42 Labour productivity growth is the rate of GDP growth minus the rate of labour force growth. TFP growth, as we have already noted, is derived from the growth accounting exercises pioneered by Solow (1956, 1957). In these exercises, the (proximate) sources of growth are the growth of factor inputs weighted according to their relative importance in the national production and a residual contribution from TFP growth.

43 Crude TFP growth averaged 0.68 per cent per year during this period. See Crafts (2021).

44 In the Huntsman's process, pieces of blister steel were placed in clay crucibles ("pots"), a flux (shards of glass) was added, and the crucibles were then heated by coke.
45 Potter (2023b, p. 2).
46 "The entire history of steel", p. 5; www.matil.org/en/news/steel-sector/the-entire-history-of-steel-1202.html.
47 Potter (2023b, p. 3). "Phosphorous content was less of a problem in wrought iron production due to lower temperatures, which prevent the phosphorous oxides from reducing back into the metal".
48 Cf. Potter (2023b).
49 Potter (2023b, p. 6).
50 See Potter (2023b, p. 7).
51 "While the Thomas-Gilchrist process did not work on the low phosphorous US ores in a Bessemer converter, the same adaptation (a basic dolomite furnace lining) in an open hearth furnace did allow the use of low phosphorous ores. This ultimately allowed open hearth costs to reach parity with Bessemer costs in the US, as cheaper sources of ore could be used".
52 The Belgian Ernest Solvay (1838–1922) revolutionised the production of sodium carbonate (soda ash) in the 1860s. While the Leblanc process (developed in the eighteenth century) uses sodium chloride, sulphuric acid, limestone and coal, the Solvay process produces soda ash from salt and limestone through the use of ammonia, which is recycled repeatedly. The Solvay process is more cost-effective and less polluting than the Leblanc process.
53 Liebig's book is entitled 'Organic Chemistry in its Application to Agriculture and Physiology' and was commissioned by the British Association for the Advancement of Sciences.
54 Potash is made of Potassium. Rock deposits bearing potash resulted when ancient inland seas evaporated millions of years ago. The term potash has been commonly used to describe the fertiliser form of potassium derived from these rocks by separating the salt and other minerals.
55 Markwood (1951, p. 351).
56 See note 52.
57 Murmann (2002, p. 4).
58 Murmann (2002, p. 5).
59 Markwood (1951, p. 350).
60 See Sanderson (1972) and Beer (1959, cited by Wengenroth 2000).
61 Murmann (2002, p. 5).
62 A generator converts mechanical energy into electrical energy.
63 dc power sends electrons in only one direction. "In a simple generator the current gets reversed when the rotor in rotating eventually turns completely around, reversing the current. Early inventors did not know what to do with this alternating current, so they invented a commutator (which

is a switch that allows current to flow in one direction". See the exposition in Edison Tech Centre: Generators & Dynamos.

64 The armature is the coil of wire windings which rotates inside the magnetic field made by the stator (the stator is a fixed structure that makes magnetic field). When the windings move, they cut through the lines of magnetic field. This creates pulses of electric power.

65 Since the magnets in a dynamo are solenoids – solenoid is a magnet created by a wire coil around an iron/ferrous core – they must be powered to work.

66 Guarnieri (2013b). See also Guarnieri (2013a).

67 This is because when electricity is transmitted over long distances, "the transmission of voltage is increased in order to reduce loses of electricity. When the electricity is sent to individual consumers transformers are needed to lower the voltage. Direct current transformers are complex and expensive, while alternating current transformers are simpler and much less expensive" (Edison Tech Centre).

68 cf. Guarnieri (2013a, 2013b).

69 From the Siemens website.

70 The "basics" of the internal combustion engine can be outlined as follows. The internal combustion engine converts fuel into mechanical energy through the combustion of fuel within a confined space, normally in cylinders. The combustion process creates high-pressure gases that drive pistons (a piston is a part of the engine that moves up and down inside the cylinder). A stroke is when the piston moves from the top centre to the bottom of the cylinder. In a four-stroke engine, the first stroke draws the fuel-air mixture into the cylinder, the second stroke compresses it, the third delivers power as the mixture explodes, and the fourth pushes the exhaust gases out of the cylinder.

In contrast, in a two-stroke engine, the cycle is completed in two strokes of the piston: the compression and ignition on the upstroke, and power and exhaust during the downstroke.

In a spark ignition engine, the fuel-air mixture is ignited by an electric spark generated by the spark plug (the spark plug being a device for generating a spark between two electrodes). In a compression ignition engine, no spark plug is used. Instead, the fuel is ignited by the high compression of the air in the combustion chamber.

71 The torque output of a motor is the amount of rotational force that the motor develops.

72 See the discussion in Chapter 2.

73 Note that these opportunities were not available to the Indian or Chinese students at that time.

74 cf. Travis (1992, p. 62).

75 cf. Guarnieri (2013b, p. 52).

76 See McCreath Laboratories, "People of Steel: Siemens and Martin".

77 GEC was a distinct business from its more famous near namesake in the USA, General Electric of America (GE).
78 cf. Jarvis (1998, p. 9).
79 The case of Germany in particular stands out in this context.
80 Railroad development in the USA and the development of steel industry in Germany can be seen as examples. In the case of railroads in the USA, the Encyclopaedia Britannica (in its discussion of the Early American railroads) puts it thus: "it seems reasonable to argue that once the British had shown that railroads could be made to work the Americans reinvented them for a very different terrain, economic climate, and demographic level". We have discussed the development of steel industry in Germany in the text above.
81 For a discussion of these reasons, see, in particular, Hoffman (2015).

References

Allen, R. C. (2009), *The British Industrial Revolution in Global Perspective*, Cambridge: Cambridge University Press.

Baines, E. (1835), *History of the Cotton Manufacture in Great Britain*, London: M. Fisher, R. Fisher, and P. Jackson.

Bakker, G., Crafts, N. and Woltjer, P. (2018), "The sources of growth in a technologically progressive economy: The United States, 1891–1941", *Economic Journal*, Vol. 129, pp. 2267–2294.

Beer, J. J. (1959), *The Emergence of the German Dye Industry*, Urbana: University of Illinois Press.

Benaerts, P. (1933), *Les Origines de la Grande Industrie Allemande*, Paris: Editions T. H. Turot.

Bulliet, R., Crossley, P. M., Hirsch, S., Johnson, L. and Northrup, D. (2023), *The Earth and its Peoples: A Global History*, Boston, MA: Cengage.

Bulstrode, J. (2023), "Black metallurgists and the making of the industrial revolution", *Science and Technology*, May (online), pp. 1–40.

Cain, P. J. and Hopkins, A. G. (2001), *British Imperialism: 1688–2000*, London: Routledge.

Cameron, R. E. (1956), "Some French contributions to the industrial development of Germany", *Journal of Economic History*, Vol. XVI, No. 3, pp. 281–321.

Clough, S. B. (1946), "Retardative factors in French economic development in the nineteenth and twentieth centuries", *Journal of Economic History*, Vol. VI, pp. 91–102.

Colebrooke, H. T. (1817), *Algebra, with Arithmetic, and Mensuration: From the Sanscrit of Brahmegupta and Bhascara*, London: John Murray.

Crafts, N. (2004), "Steam as a general purpose technology: A growth accounting perspective", *Economic Journal*, Vol. 114, pp. 338–351.

Crafts, N. (2020), "British relative economic decline in the aftermath of German unification", Warwick Economics Research Papers, No. 1295.

Crafts, N. (2021), "Understanding productivity growth in the industrial revolution", *Economic History Review*, Vol. 74, pp. 309–338.

Crafts, N. and Woltjer, P. (2021), "Growth accounting in economic history: Findings, lessons and new directions", *Journal of Economic Surveys*, Vol. 35, pp. 670–696.

Dalrymple, W. (2020), "Robert Clive was a vicious asset-stripper", *Opinion, The Guardian*, Thursday 11 June.

Darwin, J. (2008), *After Tamerlane: The Global History of Empire since 1405*, New York: Bloomsbury.

David, P. and Bunn, J. A. (1988), "The economics of gateway technologies and network evolution: Lessons from electricity supply industry", *Information Economics and Policy*, Vol. 3, pp. 165–202.

DeGroot (2024), Review of Walter Reid's "Fighting Retreat, Churchill and India", *The Times Saturday Review*, 6 January 2024.

Dunham, A. L. (1928), "The development of cotton industry in France and the Anglo-French Treaty of Commerce of 1860", *Economic History Review*, Vol. 1, No. 2, pp. 281–307.

Ellison, T. (1886), *The cotton trade of Great Britain*, London: Effingham Wilson, Royal Exchange.

Estevadeordal, A., Frantz, B. and Taylor, A. (2003), "The rise and fall of world trade, 1870–1939", *Quarterly Journal of Economics*, Vol. 118, pp. 359–407.

Federico, G. (2004), "The growth of agricultural production: 1800–1938". *Research in Economic History*, Vol. 22, pp. 125–181.

Federico, G. (2005), *Feeding the World: An Economic History of Agriculture, 1800–2000*, Princeton: Princeton University Press.

Findlay, R. and O'Rourke, K. H. (2007), *Power and Plenty: Trade, War, and the World Economy in the Second Millennium*, Princeton: Princeton University Press.

Fitzgerald, R. (2017), "International business and the development of British electrical manufacturing, 1866–1929", *The Business History Review*, Vol. 91, pp. 31–70.

Frank, A. G. (1998), *Reorient: Global Economy in the Asian Age*, Berkeley: University of California Press.

Fraser, L. (1919), *Iron and Steel in India: A Chapter from the Life of Jamshedji N. Tata*, Bombay: The Times Press.

Fremdling, R. (1991), "The German iron and steel industry in the 19th century" in Abe, E. and Suzuki, Y. (eds.), *Changing Patterns of Industrial Rivalry: Some Lessons from the Steel Industry*, Tokyo: University of Tokyo Press.

Gerschenkron, A. (1962), *Economic Backwardness in Historical Perspective*, Cambridge, MA: Harvard University Press.

Goldstone, J. A. (2002), "Efflorescences and economic growth in world history: Rethinking the 'Rise of the West' and the industrial revolution", *Journal of World History*, Vol. 13, pp. 323–389.

Goldstone, J. A. (2015), "The great and little divergence: Where lies the true onset of modern economic growth?", Working Paper. Available at SSRN: https://ssrn.com/abstract=2599287.

Goldstone, J. A. (2021), "Dating the great divergence", *Journal of Global History*, Vol. 16, pp. 260–285.

Guarnieri, M. (2013a), "The beginning of electric energy transmission: Part One", *IEEE Industrial Electronics Magazine*, Vol. 7, pp. 50–52.

Guarnieri, M. (2013b), "The beginning of electric energy transmission: Part Two", *IEEE Industrial Electronics Magazine*, Vol. 7, pp. 52–59.

Hacker, B. (1977), "The weapons of the west: Military technology and modernisation in the 19th century China and Japan", *Technology and Culture*, Vol. 18, No. 1, pp. 43–55.

Harley, C. K. (1988), "Ocean freight rates and productivity 1740–1913: The primacy of mechanical innovation reaffirmed", *Journal of Economic History*, Vol. 48, No. 4, pp. 851–876.

Harris, J. R. (1988), *The British Iron Industry*, Basingstoke: Macmillan.

Hilden, P. (1993), "Belgium, 1795–1914", Chapter 2 of *Women, Work and Politics: Belgium 1830–1914*, Oxford: Oxford University Press.

Hoffman, P. (2015), *Why Did Europe Conquer the World?*, Princeton: Princeton University Press.

Hume, D. (1748), "Of national characters", Essay XXI in *Essays, Moral, Political, and Literary*, Part 1, Edinburgh: A. Kincaid.

Hyde, C. K. (1979), *Technological Change and the British Iron Industry, 1700–1870*, Princeton: Princeton University Press.

Inikori, J. E. (2002), *Africans and the Industrial Revolution in England: A Study in International Trade and Economic Development*, Cambridge: Cambridge University Press.

Jarvis, A. (1998), "The nineteenth-century roots of globalisation: Some technological considerations" in Starkey, D. and Harlaftis, G. (eds.), *Global Markets: The Internationalisation of Sea Transport Industries since 1850*, Oxford: Oxford University Press.

Juhasz, R. (2018), "Temporary protection and technology adoption: Evidence from the Napoleonic blockade", *American Economic Review*, Vol. 108, pp. 3339–3376.

Kant, I. (1803), *Physische Geographic*, Mainz, Hamburg: G. Vollmer.

Kaukiainen, Y. (2001), "Shrinking the world: Improvements in the speed of information transmission, c. 1820–1870", *European Review of Economic History*, Vol. 5, pp. 1–28.

Kendrick, J. W. (1961), *Productivity Trends in the United States*, Princeton: Princeton University Press.

Kobayashi, K. (2018), "The British Atlantic slave trade and Indian cotton textiles: The case of Thomas Lumley & Co.", Chapter 3 of Shiroyama, T. (ed.), *Modern Global Trade and the Asian Regional Economy*, pp. 59–85, Japan: Monograph Series of Socio-Economic History Society.

Konig, W. (1996), "Science-based industry or industry-based science? Electrical engineering in Germany before World War 1", *Technology and Culture*, Vol. 37, pp. 70–101.

Kuppuram, G. and Kumudamani, K. (1990), *History of Science and Technology in India*, Delhi: Sundeep Prakashan.

Landes, D. S. (1949), "French entrepreneurship and industrial growth in the nineteenth century", *Journal of Economic History*, Vol. IX, pp. 45–61.

Landes, D. S. (2006), "Why Europe and the West? Why not China", *Journal of Economic Perspective*, Vol. 20, pp. 3–22.

Lee, J. and Wang, F. (1999), *One Quarter of Humanity: Malthusian Mythology and Chinese Realities, 1700–2000*, Cambridge, MA: Harvard University Press.

Lewis, W. A. (1949), *The Principles of Economic Planning*, London: Routledge.

Lewis, W. A. (1952), "World production, prices and trade, 1870–1950", *The Manchester School*, Vol. 20, pp. 105–138.

Lewis, W. A. (1981), "The rate of growth of world trade 1870–1913" in Grossman, S. and Lundberg, E. (eds.), *The World Economic Order: Past and Prospects*, pp. 11–74, London and Basingstoke: Macmillan.

Liebig, J. (1840), Die Organische Chemic in ihres Anwendung auf Agricultur und Physiologie, Commissioned by the British Association for the Advancement of Sciences.

MacLeod, C. (2004), "The European origins of British technological predominance" in Escosura, L. P. (ed.), *Exceptionalism and Industrialisation: Britain and its European Rivals 1688–1815*, pp. 111–126, Cambridge: Cambridge University Press.

Malanima, P. (2001), "The energy basis for early modern growth, 1650–1829" in Prak, M. (ed.), *Early Modern Capitalism: Economic and Social Change in Europe 1400–1800*, London: Routledge.

Markwood, L. N. (1951), "European chemical industry in the nineteenth century" [A Symposium presented at the 118th Meeting of the American Chemical Society, Chicago, September 5, 1950], *Journal of Chemical Education*, July, pp. 348–352.

McCloskey, D. N. (2010), *Bourgeois Dignity: Why Economics Can't Explain the Modern World*, Chicago: University of Chicago Press.

Mohammed, S. I. S. and Williamson, J. G. (2004), "Freight rates and productivity gains in British tramp shipping 1869–1950", *Explorations in Economic History*, Vol. 41, No. 2, pp. 172–203.

Mokyr, J. (2002), *The Gifts of Athena*, Princeton: Princeton University Press.

Mokyr, J. (2003), "Accounting for the industrial revolution" in Johnson, P. and Floud, R. (eds.), *The Cambridge Economic History of Britain*, Cambridge: Cambridge University Press.

Morris, I. (2010), *Why the West Rules – for Now: The Patterns of History and What They Reveal about the Future*, London: Profile.

Murmann, J. P. (2002), "Chemical Industries after 1850" in *Oxford Encyclopaedia of Economic History*, Oxford: Oxford University Press.

Needham, J. (1954–), *Science and Civilisation in China*, Cambridge: Cambridge University Press.

Needham, J. (1964), "Science and China's influence in the world" in Dawson, R. (ed.), *The Legacy of China*, Oxford: Clarendon Press.

Parthasarathi, P. (2011), *Why Europe Grew Rich and Asia Did Not: Global Economic Divergence, 1600–1850*, Cambridge: Cambridge University Press.

Pomeranz, K. (2000), *The Great Divergence: China, Europe, and the Making of the Modern World Economy*, Princeton, NJ: Princeton University Press.

Potter, B. (2023a), "The rise of steel, part 1", www.construction-physics.com.

Potter, B. (2023b), "The rise of steel, part 2", www.construction-physics.com.

Poulson, B. (1994), *Economic Development: Private and Public Choice*, New York: West Publishing.

Rahman, A. (ed.) (1984), *Science and Technology in Indian Culture: A Historical Perspective*, New Delhi: National Institute of Science, Technology and Development Studies.

Reid, W. (2023), *Fighting Retreat: Churchill and India*, London: Hurst.

Riello, G. (2010), *"The making of a global commodity: Indian cottons and European trade, 1450–1850"*, World History Studies and World History Education: The Proceedings of the First Congress of the Asian Association of World Historians.

Sanderson, M. (1972), *The Universities and British Industry, 1850–1970*, London: Routledge and Keegan.

Singh, P. (1985), "The so-called Fibonacci numbers in ancient and medieval India", *Historica Mathematica, Academic Press*, Vol. 12, pp. 229–244.

Solow, R. (1956), "A contribution to the theory of economic growth", *Quarterly Journal of Economics*, Vol. 70, pp. 65–94.

Solow, R. (1957), "Technical change and the aggregate production function", *Review of Economics and Statistics*, Vol. 39, pp. 312–320.

Spence, J. D. (1996), *God's Chinese Son: The Taiping Heavenly Kingdom of Hong Xiuquan*, New York: W. W. Norton.

Srinivasan, S. and Ranganathan, S. (2004), *India's Legendary Wootz Steel*, Bangalore: Tata Steel.

Tainter, J. A. (1988), *The Collapse of Complex Societies*, Cambridge: Cambridge University Press.

Tawney, R. H. (1926), *Religion and the Rise of Capitalism*, New York: Harcourt Brace and World.

Temin, P. (1966), "Labour scarcity and the problem of American industrial efficiency in the 1850s", *Journal of Economic History*, Vol. 26, pp. 277–298.

Tharoor, S. (2016), *Inglorious Empire: What the British Did to India*, London: Penguin.

Travis, A. S. (1992), "August Wilhelm Hofmann (1818–1892)", *Endeavour, New Series*, Vol. 16, pp. 59–65.

Tunzelman, N. (2003), "Technology" in Mokyr, J. (ed.), *The Oxford Encyclopaedia of Economic History*, Oxford: Oxford University Press.

Weber, M. (1905), *The Protestant Ethic and the Spirit of Capitalism*, London: Routledge.

Wengenroth, U. (2000), "Science, technology, and industry in the 19th century", Working Paper, Munich Centre for the History of Science and Technology.

Yates, C. (2017), "Five ways ancient India changed the world – with maths", *The Conversation*, 21 September, pp. 1–5.

4 Silver and slavery

Introduction

In the preceding two chapters we have emphasised the role of India in the rise of Europe and the emergence of modern economic growth. It may be of some interest to consider also, first, the role of the greatly increased supply of silver coins in the sixteenth and seventeenth centuries following the discovery of huge deposits of silver in Mexico and Peru, and second, that of the Atlantic slave trade. Both have been mentioned in the literature as having been of importance for the rise of Europe.

Adam Smith had written that "the discovery of America, and that of the passage to the East Indies by the Cape of Good Hope, are the two greatest and most important events in the history of mankind …" (The Wealth of Nations, pp. 590–591). The "discovery" of America, besides leading to the discovery of silver deposits, also led to the destruction of its people and the beginnings of forced and slave labour in the Americas and to the Atlantic slave trade. We shall briefly sketch out the historical background of these events at the same time as we try to weigh up their importance for the rise of Europe.

Spain and Portugal in the Americas

From the early fifteenth century, the Portuguese had been trading down the west coast of Africa for slaves, gold, pepper and ivory. Their great achievement during the period of discovery was the finding of the sea route to India via the Cape by Vasco da Gama (the voyage of 1497–1499), and for the next several decades the Portuguese effort was concentrated on their Asian trade. The Dutch and the English East

DOI: 10.4324/9781003715368-4

India Companies joined the Asian trade in the early seventeenth century. The Dutch displaced the Portuguese in the Spice Islands of Tidor and Tennate, and Java; the English East India Company (EEIC), after failing to dislodge the Dutch from the Spice Islands and Java, based itself in India for its trading activities. EEIC's subsequent control of Bengal and its land revenue in the mid-eighteenth century was, as we have already seen, to be the springboard for the British in dominating the world economy and shaping its evolution.

Portugal's pre-occupation with finding a sea route to India meant that America fell to Spain, not Portugal. Indeed, Portugal's seamen would often call at Brazil on their Indian voyages. Yet, Columbus' discovery of America in 1492 rested squarely on Portugal's experience in seafaring. Columbus had approached the Portuguese court first; being rebuffed there, he came to the Spanish court to seek support for his mission, and with the Spanish patronage he landed in the Bahamas in 1492. The Treaty of Tordesillas (1494) subsequently divided the Americas between Spain and Portugal, giving Portugal its title to Brazil (where the Portuguese came to grow sugar with slave labour; later the discovery of gold at various points in Minas Geraes and further west was also to prove important).[1] For the next one hundred years, Spain and Portugal were the only countries with well-established presence in Americas.

For some 20 years after Columbus' first voyage the Spanish presence in America was limited mainly to the West Indies and mainly to one island, Hispaniola. The New World's first Spanish city, Santo Domingo, was founded there in 1496. By 1500 Hispaniola had a white population of only one thousand (all males). As the number of immigrants increased, they ventured outwards in search of slaves and land. Warfare, forced labour, and epidemic had brought about the near extinction of the original Taino inhabitants of Hispaniola. According to Bartolome' de Las Casas, the sixteenth-century Spanish historian, three million Tainos perished between 1494 and 1508. In search of labour, the settlers made slaving raids on neighbouring islands. In the process they also settled the islands: Puerto Rico from 1508, Cuba from 1511 and Jamaica from 1513. Cuban and Puerto Rican populations, too, met the same fate as the Tainos.

There was little settlement on the mainland until Hernan Cortes' landing on the Mexican coast in 1529 opened two years of campaigning in which he overthrew the Aztec Empire. This was followed by the overthrow of the Peruvian Empire of the Incas by Francisco Pizarro in

1532–1533. Spain concentrated attention, from this time onwards, in the two thickly populated regions of Peru and central Mexico, regions with settled peasantry and producers of a surplus that was simply transferred to new rulers.

The practice of *encomienda* (commendation) was instituted as a model for Spaniard's relation with a subject race. Under the practice the Indian villagers were put under the "protection" of individual Spaniards (*encomenderos*), who in return were entitled to performance of some services for them by their village Indians and to receive tribute in gold and other goods. However, the labour structure in the Indies was soon collapsing under the impact of demographic catastrophe. As Spaniards penetrated the remote territories they brought with them new viruses, particularly smallpox, to which the natives had no immunity and which caused devastating epidemics. The unaccustomed labour obligations, the wholesale disruption of communities, and the cruelties of the Spaniards also had their effects. In central Mexico the Indian population declined rapidly from about 25.2 million in 1518 to 2.65 million in 1568 and just over one million in 1605; in Peru a pre-conquest population of about nine million fell to some 600,000 in 1620. As the workforce shrank, the encomiendas became impractical: the authorities stepped in and organised a system, known in Mexico as the *repartimiento* and in Peru by the pre-Spanish term *mita,* by which available labour was leased out to estate owners for limited periods (for further discussions, see, among others, Kamen 2003, 2014).

Meanwhile, African slaves were being imported to meet the labour needs. Slave trade made its first landing in America as early as 1503, but large shipments began after 1518 when sugar plantations were being established on the lands round the town of Santo Domingo. Portugal supplied the slaves to their own colony of Brazil as well as to Spaniards. By the 1560s there were more blacks than whites in Hispaniola, Mexico City, Lima and throughout Spanish America. (In 1574, there were some 1500 Spaniards in the islands, mostly in Hispaniola, and some thousands of African slaves).

Slavery and forced labour were integral to the overseas expansion of Europe from the very beginning.

Discovery of silver deposits and the influx of bullions

One of the major consequences of the Spanish penetration in the New World was the discovery in Mexico and Peru of rich deposits of gold and especially silver. Silver was the main base for currency in most monetised societies at that time. There was, therefore, the need for an adequate supply of silver as a means of exchange. Silver had always flowed out of Europe into Asia. Euro-Asian trade had traditionally been one involving the exchange of Asian goods mainly against European silver and, to a smaller extent, gold. This "bullion for goods" pattern of trade was a consequence of the inability of Europe to supply goods that could be sold in Asia in reasonably large quantities in competitive terms. As a result, Europe really had no option but to pay for the Asian goods overwhelmingly in terms of precious metals.[2] Apart from this "leakage" to Asia, silver disappeared too into non-monetary uses, for religious and lay ornament, into hoards, and in the ordinary wear of coin. Medieval production of silver was not adequate to meet the demand for its various uses. The problem had somewhat eased with the expansion of central European production late in the fifteenth century and the arrival of American silver in some quantities from the 1530s. However, it was in 1552 that the first great cargoes from the new American mines arrived in Spain.[3] From that year "the import of American silver rapidly mounted to reach a peak of some seven million ounces a year in the last decade of the century, maintaining this level until the 1620s. There was again a huge surge in silver inflow around 1665–1700, probably considerably greater in quantity than the amount reached in the last decades of the sixteenth century" (see, e.g., Kamen 2003). These figures may be compared with a central European production of half a million ounces a year at its peak in the 1630s.

What then were the major effects of this influx of silver? About 20 per cent of the metal went to the Spanish Crown directly. This immediately translated itself to an increased demand for military services and for arms and provisions by the Crown, obsessed as the Crown was with the idea of a Catholic Crusade. There were payments to the Crown's foreign creditors, for the Crown was perpetually in debt from involvements in numerous wars (most of which Spain lost). Most of the rest of the silver that came to Spain went first to other parts of Europe to purchase goods and services of various kinds. As has been said, Spain became richer but did not develop or lay the basis for sustainable development. Cipolla (1976) quotes the Venetian Ambassador Vendramin commenting thus: "about this precious metal which comes to Spain from the Indies, the Spaniards say not without reason that it falls on Spain as does rain on a roof – it pours on her and then flows away". The Spanish demand, sustained by American silver, promoted the economic development of Holland, England, France and other European countries. "Northern Europe, in particular, benefitted greatly, for Spain depended on the north for wheat, copper, tin, wood, planks, beams, hemp and linen cloth, and for high-quality textiles. The Dutch shipping, in particular, brought corn and other Baltic produce, and Spanish silver was carried away in great quantities to Amsterdam, which by 1650s had become Europe's chief bullion market". It has been said that the inflow of American bullion explains the rise to power of the urban merchant class in Europe which grew in strength as the volume of trade increased. In England a great deal of silver came through privateering and this – according to Keynes (1930) – gave fillip to enterprises of all kinds.

The increase in the stock of money and the increased demand for goods and services of various kinds are thought to have led to what is referred to as the Price Revolution. Between the second half of the sixteenth century and the first half of the seventeenth century, prices rose consistently in many countries (when compounded, the estimated annual rate of inflation over the period has been put at between 1 and 1.6 per cent – a modest rate of growth by the present-day standards but considered highly significant in the context of developments then).[4] It has been claimed further that while the wages too rose, the prices rose faster than wages, so that there was an increase in profits for the entrepreneurs and this then led to an increase in capital accumulation and economic expansion. Hamilton (1934) has been an early and forceful champion of this view, a view that has also been endorsed by Keynes (1930). Others have demurred. This has been a field of much controversy, with some arguing that the price rise was due to the increased population growth during this period rather than due to the increase in the influx of silver (see, e.g., Chambers 1972; Goldstone 1991; Fischer 1996), while still others arguing that both the population growth and the inflow of precious metals were jointly responsible for the rise in prices (see Edo and Melitz 2019).

What is not in dispute, however, is the fact that the inflow of silver from the Americas led to an increase in Europe's trade with Asia. Euro-Asian trade, as we have just noted, had predominantly been one of bullions for goods. Silver was also needed for various East India companies' intra-Asian trade.[5] Parthasarathi (2011, pp. 46–50) has estimated that between 1600 and 1800 roughly a fifth of world production of silver flowed into the Indian subcontinent, mainly to pay for the huge quantity of Indian cotton textiles bought on the world market.[6] The inflow of silver to China was even larger. There was a huge demand for Chinese porcelain, silk and other commodities in the world market. Since China desired little as imports from other countries, the Chinese goods had to be paid for by silver. Domestic monetary developments in China were also important. China was establishing a monetary system based on silver following the failed experiments with paper money in the late Ming period. Silver was consequently in great demand and reliable arbitrage profits could be made by sending silver to China.

The influx of bullions would thus appear to have had a number of important consequences: it led to an increase in the demand for the products of a number of countries; it possibly led to some capital accumulation via profit inflation in some of the countries and certainly led to an increase in trade with Asia (and trade generally). It helped to link together the various parts of the world via trade.

But how important was this trade, especially Europe's trade with Asia on which so much attention has been devoted in the literature? De Vries (2010, p. 9) has provided estimates of all European Cape-route trade with Asia over the period 1501–1795: "In the aggregate, the Europe-Asia trade was remarkably stable, growing at an annual rate of 1.10 percent across the three early modern centuries, and growing at very nearly that rate in each of the three centuries separately … . A 1.10 percent annual rate of growth sustained over 300 years yields an impressive total increase in the volume of trade: 25 fold. But does this deserve to be called a 'boom'? At the end of this long era, the total volume of goods sent annually from all of Asia to all of Europe measured approximately 50,000 tons – the carrying capacity of one large container ship of today".

De Vries also found that the European trading companies' profits from the Europe-Asian trade were generally not high and became less so over time. Profits from participation in intra-Asian trade were probably higher for a time, especially for the Dutch East India Company (VOC). It was only after the colonisation that trading revenue could be supplemented and substituted for by political revenue.

So what can we say about the role of the influx of bullions in the emergence of modern economic growth? One cannot, of course, be certain, but given that – and as we have noted in Chapter 1 – the emergence of modern economic growth was sudden, that the past growth patterns did not matter for the emergence of modern economic growth, that there was, as it were, a structural break in GDP/cap growth path around 1800 or even later, it would appear unlikely that the injections of precious metals in the world economy in the sixteenth and seventeenth centuries[7] could have on their own led to the sustained high GDP/cap growth path that started in Britain in the early nineteenth century.

As against the above assessment, however, one may wish to weigh up the impact of demonstration effects of the imported Asian goods. These goods brought to Europe new needs and the incentive to produce them at home. As Abbe Raynal (1776) wrote: "If Saxony and other countries of Europe make up the China, if Valencia manufactures Pekins superior to those of China; if Switzerland imitates the muslins and worked calicoes of Bengal; if England and France print linens with great elegance; if so many stuffs, formerly unknown in our climates, now employ our best artists, are we not indebted to India for all these advantages?" Within a few years, of course, Raynal would not have failed to mention the most successful imitators of the Indians, Manchester.

It has also been argued (see de Vries 2008) that the availability of imported and novel Asian goods led to consumers in Europe aspiring to acquire them, and they therefore increased their work efforts to be able to acquire them. "This resulted in an 'industrious revolution' that led to higher incomes and specialisation". As against this optimistic view, however, others have suggested that the increase in work efforts – if indeed this is what happened – may have had more to do with a decline in real wages in the second half of the eighteenth century than with any rising consumer aspirations (see Motavvasseli and Smulders 2017).

So we conclude on an agnostic note. We acknowledge that the influx of bullions may have had beneficial effects on economic development in some of the countries. It certainly led to the globalisation of trade. However, we remain less than convinced that this globalisation of trade in the sixteenth century alone did or could have led to continuing technological innovations and therefore to a sustained high GDP/cap growth path that – as the evidence now suggests – started only from the early nineteenth century.

The Atlantic slave trade, Britain and the technologies of the First Industrial Revolution

Having discussed the role of the influx of bullions, we now turn to a discussion of the role of the Atlantic slave trade. In discussing the

Atlantic slave trade, we shall focus our attention on Britain. Britain was the predominant slave trader in the Western hemisphere from around 1660 to 1807 (when Parliament outlawed British participation in slave-carrying). Britain was also, of course, the first country to industrialise. (It is, however, important to remember in this context that Britain was not unique in having slave trade.)

Carriers of slaves

The Portuguese had dominated the Atlantic slave trade throughout the sixteenth century. The Dutch then came to dominate the trade. The English had entered the slave trade relatively late, but by 1670 they had become the leading carrier of slaves across the Atlantic and remained so until 1807. "Overall, it appears that in the one-and-a-half centuries before 1807 the British shipped as many slaves to America as all other slave-carrying nations put together. In 1660–1807, therefore, the British were the pre-eminent slave traders of the western hemisphere" (Richardson 1998). During the period 1662–1807, the British shipped a little over 3.4 million slaves from Africa to America.

The British participation in slave trade – as we have just mentioned – was abolished by an enactment of British Parliament in 1807 (more on this below). Most European powers, with the exception of Spain and Portugal, had enacted similar legislation by 1821. However, despite its legal abolition in a number of countries, the African slave trade was growing rapidly in the early decades of the nineteenth century, and by 1840 it was estimated to have been double what it had been in 1807.[8] The transatlantic slave trade continued well into the 1860s; the major post-1820 recipients of slaves were Brazil and the Spanish Caribbean colonies, particularly Cuba.

Impact of the slave trade and slave labour on the British economic development

The profits that the British earned from the Atlantic slave trade have been the subject of much debate. Some historians – most notably Williams (1944) – have claimed that profits from the slave trade made a major contribution to the financing of the industrial revolution in Britain. This, however, has been disputed by others. Richardson (2003) – a leading researcher in the area – has put it thus: "comparison between earnings from slave voyages with general estimates of eighteenth-century British investment generally suggests, almost without exception, that slave-trading profits could have contributed at best only small amounts to financing early British industrial expansion". He gives the following as an illustration: "Investment in slaving voyages in Britain probably exceeded £1.5 million a year around 1790 and perhaps yielded £150,000 a year in profits. Assuming £50,000 of this was invested in new enterprises, profits from the slave trade, therefore, probably contributed under 1 per cent of total domestic investment in Britain at this time" (Richardson 1998). Such calculations do not suggest that the slave trade profit was crucial for the financing of early British industrial expansion. It is also disputed whether the profits from the slave trade and the plantation system were in fact higher than those from other (domestic) sectors of the economy and whether these profits were actually invested in those sectors crucial to the Industrial Revolution, viz., the iron, coal and textile industries (Eltis and Engerman 2000).

However, in assessing the impact of the slave trade on Britain's economy, we need to go beyond the profitability of the trade itself. Slavery underpinned the whole of Britain's trading empire in America. In this trading network, Britain supplied manufactured goods and capital, West Africa slave labour (slaves obtained from African slave traders in exchange, mainly for textiles, guns and gun powder), the southern colonies and the West Indies sugar, tobacco and other plantation products (especially rice and indigo) in exchange mainly for manufactured goods from Britain. Other mainland colonies financed imports of manufactured goods from Britain by selling flour, grains and meat to West Indian plantations and with income earned from shipping and commercial activities in Philadelphia and New York. Daniel Defoe, writing in his Review of 10 January 1711, summed up the various links connecting this network as follows: "*No African* trade, *no* Negroes; *no* Negroes, *no* Sugars, Ginger, Indigos, &c*; no* Sugars, &c., *no* Islands; *no* Islands, *no* Continent; *no* Continent, *no* trade; that is to say, farewell all your *American* Trade, your *West-India* Trade …"

But how important was this trade though? On the import side, sugar produced by slaves became Britain's single largest item of imports. After 1630, English West Indies colonies had become essentially sugar cane monocultures. While in 1700 they exported 22,000 tons of sugar to England and Wales, this had risen to 41,425 tons in 1748, and to 164,859 tons in 1815. Sugar remained Britain's largest single import from the 1750s, when it overtook foreign linen, until the 1820s, when it was surpassed by raw cotton (again produced by slaves, this time in the American South). Sugar duties usually accounted for about an eighth of the exchequer revenue. Further, tea in combination with sugar was to become the national drink, with important economic and health benefits.[9]

On the export side, Britain exported mostly textiles, guns and a variety of metal goods to her colonies in America and to the slave traders in West Africa. There has been a good deal of discussion in the literature on the impact of this trade on British economic development. Regarding Britain's trade with her American colonies, McCusker and Menard (1991), after a careful analysis of the period 1607–1789, concluded thus: "The profits earned in colonial trades were not unusually high; ... did not engender major processing industries in the metropolis and did little to stimulate the economy as a whole. Throughout our period, colonial markets for British manufactures were generally small, seldom accounting for more than 20 per cent of the output of any industry, and were generally overshadowed by the home market. Furthermore, British industries that were directly dependent on colonial trade – shipping, for instance – were relatively minor" (p. 77). Similarly, Eltis and Engerman (2000) concluded: "If the value added and strategic linkages of the sugar industry are compared to those of other British industries, it is apparent that sugar cultivation and the slave trade were not particularly large, nor did they have stronger growth-inducing ties with the rest of the British economy".

But what of the argument that the increased demand for manufactured goods from her trading partners in the Atlantic world led to technological innovations in Britain? While the growth of British population and of exports to Europe were relatively slow for most of the eighteenth century, the population of the American colonies and their demand for manufactured goods grew rapidly. Inikori (2002) in particular has argued that the growing demand for cotton cloth and metal goods in the Atlantic world caused the technical breakthrough in the textile and metal industries in Britain. So far as the cotton textile industry is concerned, we have already noted in the last chapter some of the other explanations that have been offered in the literature to explain the mechanisation of cotton textile industry in Britain, and we have expressed our reservations about the Inikori hypothesis there. In any case, it would seem reasonable to suggest that the innovations in the cotton textile industry alone would not have been sufficient to ensure that growth (and innovations) would not have petered out at some point in future in the absence of further technological innovations elsewhere. Inikori provides no mechanism to explain how growth and technological innovations could have become a continuing process.

The same reservations apply with respect of the argument regarding innovations in the metal industries. Minchinton (1969) has provided a survey of British overseas trade over the period 1688–1772. Demand for the products of metal industry certainly grew abroad, and particularly in the American colonies in the course of the eighteenth century. "Nails, pots and pans, axes and ploughshares, kitchen and dairy utensils, buttons and buckles, anchors and other ship's ware were among the articles sent overseas". Similarly, Davis (1969) writes, "the largest group of exports outside textiles were made up by metals and their manufactures. In the eighteenth century most of the output of metalwares had been the product of handicraft industries making small objects of many kinds for household, workshop or farm use, for military purposes or for ornamentation". Native sources of metallic ores were generally adequate – there were iron, copper, zinc, lead and tin ores in Britain. As we have noted in the last chapter, iron was at first imported because of the high costs of smelting and refining with charcoal, but the spread of the general use of coke in the making of pig iron, from the 1750s onwards, and the innovations of Cort in 1784 for making wrought iron, made Britain self-sufficient.

We have also discussed in the last chapter the reasons behind the innovations in the iron industry in Britain. We concluded that a shortage of wood, a rise in the price of charcoal, an abundance of coal and iron ores (both situated closely together), the need of the army and the navy, the state mercantilist policies, and some borrowing of key technologies from abroad were all important factors behind the innovations in the iron industry.

So where does the overseas demand for "iron-made goods" fit into the picture? It is important to note that the American and West Indies colonies were not so much interested in pig iron or bar iron – "the northern colonies being in a position to export such iron to" Britain, as Harris (1988) noted – but in goods made of iron such as hardware products and nails. "Some of the iron produced in Britain was particularly well adapted" for producing these items. Nails were a major export item. For example, they accounted for over 35 per cent of the total tonnage of "worked-up or manufactured iron" during the period 1700–1709 and 21 per cent as late as 1750–1759 (see the table on p. 52 of Harris 1988). As Harris wrote, "cheap coal and a suitable home-produced iron were the main influences behind the great export of the nails made in thousands of little forges by nailmaking families" (Harris 1988, p. 52).

It would thus appear that no great technological advances were needed for meeting the demand for "iron-made goods" coming from the overseas markets. One therefore presumes that the case that is being made for viewing the technological innovations in the iron industry as having been an outcome of the overseas demand for "iron-made goods" is based on the premise that this additional demand for iron-made goods coming from the overseas markets – by creating additional demand for the metal iron itself – led to a rise in the price of charcoal and the price of "iron-made goods" generally; this then encouraged import substitution and technological innovations in the iron industry. If this indeed is the case that is being made, then it is obviously important to know how large a component this overseas demand was of the total demand for the metal iron. Minchinton (1969) has cited authorities to show that in the first half of the eighteenth century, home demand for iron was much greater than export demand. But the available figures also imply that export demand was growing faster than home demand and that "the proportion of total English iron supplies exported rose from 8 per cent in 1715–19 to 16 per cent in 1748–52, this trend continuing in the following quarter of a century and exports accounting for something of the order of 20 per cent of total English iron production in 1770".

So the overseas demand was a significant – but not an overwhelming – proportion of the total demand for the metal iron. It is, therefore, possible that even in the absence of this overseas demand, technological innovations in the iron industry could have taken place. All of the reasons that we have mentioned above as being behind the technological innovations in the iron industry would presumably still have been present even in the absence of the overseas demand for iron-made goods. But we cannot, of course, be certain. However, if we are to accept the proposition that this overseas demand played a major role in initiating modern economic growth (which has been characterised by continuing technological innovations), then the various links in the chain of causation leading to this outcome would need to be spelled out. This is yet to be done.[10]

Outlawing of the British participation in slave-carrying

By the beginning of the nineteenth century, sugar production in the West Indies was becoming less and less profitable. This was so for a number of reasons. As the number of absentee plantation owners increased, increasing amount of capital left the islands, and there was a deterioration in estate management. There was at the same time increased competition from the better organised French islands of Guadeloupe and Martinique and from Cuba and Brazil. These facts have led some historians, including Williams (1944), to conclude that the decline of the sugar industry in the British West Indies played a more important role in the abolition of slavery than the efforts of hypocritical philanthropists in Great Britain. Williams has argued that once British West Indian sugar could no longer compete successfully with sugar produced by others, the British launched an international campaign against slavery in order to ruin their French and Spanish rivals and ensure that British East Indian sugar, not dependent on slave labour, captured the European market. It is a controversial thesis. There is no doubt that the efforts of the philanthropists were genuine and sincere. It would also appear, however, that the Parliament did not believe that the country would lose greatly by giving up the slave trade at that point.

Be that as it may, the British participation in slave trade was abolished by an enactment of the British Parliament in 1807. Although British involvement in the slave trade formally ended in 1807, systems of slavery that exploited African labour remained major influences on British overseas trade and colonial history well into the nineteenth century. For one, British merchants continued to supply goods to other slave traders. For another, British cotton textile industry continued to draw around 75 per cent of its raw material from the slave states of America. The actual abolition of slavery itself in the British Empire came following the Emancipation Act in 1833. On 1 August 1834 all slaves became free, although ex-slaves over six years old were required to continue working as "apprentices" to their former masters for another six years. By this time, British had also, of course, firmly established themselves in India and indentured labourers from India would be imported to fill the labour shortage resulting from the abolition of slavery.

Conclusion

This chapter has examined the role of both the greatly increased supply of silver coins in the sixteenth and seventeenth centuries (following the discovery of huge deposits of silver in Mexico and Peru) and the Atlantic slave trade in the emergence of modern economic growth. The influx of silver is said to have led to the so-called Price Revolution, when prices rose for nearly a century or so in many countries. Others have argued that the increase in prices was instead due to the increased population growth during this period. Yet others have suggested that the increase in prices was due to a combination of both of these factors, i.e., due to both the increased availability of silver and the increased population growth. In any case, it would appear that the increase in prices, by present-day standards, was not particularly high – the estimates of the increase range between 1 and 1.6 per cent per annum over the period. It has also been claimed that the prices rose faster than wages so that there was an increase in profits for the entrepreneurs and that this led to an increase in investment by them. There have been considerable debates and disagreements surrounding these issues in the literature. What is not in dispute is the fact that the increased availability of silver led to an increase in trade, especially Europe's trade with Asia (where the bullions for goods pattern of trade predominated). While the available quantitative evidence shows that the volume of Europe's trade with Asia was not particularly large, many of the goods imported from Asia clearly had important demonstration effects and gave stimulus to their production in Europe. The influx of silver undoubtedly led to the globalisation of trade. However, we can see no obvious pathways by which this globalisation of trade alone would have been sufficient to set up a mechanism for growth and technological innovations to be a continuing process (as would be necessary for us to call the growth "modern"). We therefore remain agnostic about the precise effects of the influx of silver in the sixteenth and seventeenth centuries on the emergence of modern economic growth in a small group of countries in Western Europe and the USA in the nineteenth century.

So far as the Atlantic slave trade is concerned, this trade underpinned the whole of Britain's trading empire in America. It is also the case that the volume of Europe's Atlantic trade was at least twice the volume of Europe's Asian trade. Profits from the slave trade itself would appear not to have been particularly high. Goods imported from and exported to her American colonies would appear not to have generated strong forward or backward linkages in any of the industries involved in Britain. It has, however, been claimed by some that the demand for cotton textiles and metal goods from her American colonies and West Africa (where cotton textiles were bartered for slaves) led to technological innovations in these industries in Britain. There are, however, other explanations that have been offered in the literature for the technological innovations in these industries in Britain, and these we have discussed in the last chapter.

Notes

1 See note 7.
2 At earlier times, the Vikings and then the Venetian and Genoese merchants had also trafficked people from Europe to Asia to obtain Asian goods in exchange. See, in particular, Frankopan (2015, Chapter 7). Indeed, it is interesting to speculate whether or not this slave trade from Europe to Asia would have continued/resumed (and this at the same time as when the African slaves were being transported across the Atlantic) if silver deposits had not been discovered in Mexico and Peru.
3 Gold, whose supply had become relatively plentiful by the late fifteenth century, was not an adequate substitute for silver in an era of silver standards.
4 Especially as inflations were based on commodity money rather than government-issued fiat money.
5 Often referred to as the "country trade" in the literature.
6 Parthasarathi (2011) has also shown that the assumption by Frank (1998) and others that the bulk of the silver that flowed into India was re-exported to China is incorrect.
7 or for that matter gold in the eighteenth century. In addition to these effects of the inflow of silver from Peru and Mexico, there were also the further windfall benefits from the discovery of gold in Brazil. Throughout the first 50 years of the eighteenth century an average of 350,000 ounces of gold came annually from Brazil to Portugal. (This may be contrasted with the figure of some 7 million ounces of silver that came annually to Spain throughout most of the seventeenth century). While the principal beneficiaries of this discovery of gold were Brazil and Portugal, many other countries also experienced an inflow of gold, Britain in particular. Britain's large favourable trade balance with Portugal was settled in bullions from Brazil and this contributed to the financing of imports of iron, timber and naval stores from the Baltic. However, nobody has suggested that this inflow of gold set up a mechanism for technological innovations to be a continuing process.
8 See Kenwood and Locheed (1983): the increase was from 100,000 to 200,000 a year, of whom 150,000 were carried across the Atlantic and 50,000 went to the Arab world.
9 Note that there is a strong Indian connection in all of this: sugar being produced by slaves, slaves being obtained in exchange partly for Indian cotton textiles; tea being obtained from China in exchange for Indian opium smuggled into China.

10 There may, of course, be a final twist here. As already noted, Bulstrode (2023) has recently argued that the innovations usually credited to Cort were in fact due to black Jamaican metallurgists – some of whom were slaves. See note 30 of Chapter 3.

References

Abbe Raynal (1776), *A Philosophical and Political History of Settlements and Trade of the Europeans in the East and West Indies*, London: Printed for T. Cadell.

Bulstrode, J. (2023), "Black metallurgists and the making of the industrial revolution", *Science and Technology*, May (online), pp. 1–40.

Chambers, J. D. (1972), *Population, Economy and Society in Pre-industrial England*, Oxford: Oxford University Press.

Cipolla, C. M. (1976), *Before the Industrial Revolution: European Society and Economy 1000–1700*, London: Methuen.

Davis, R. (1969), "English foreign trade: 1700–1774", Chapter 3 in Minchinton, W. (ed.), *The Growth of English Overseas Trade in the Seventeenth and Eighteenth Centuries*, London: Routledge.

De Vries, J. (2008), *The Industrial Revolution: Consumer Behaviour and the Household Economy*, Cambridge: Cambridge University Press.

De Vries, J. (2010), "The limits of globalisation in the early modern world", *Economic History Review*, Vol. 63, pp. 710–733.

Edo, A. and Melitz, J. (2019), "The primary cause of European inflation in 1500–1700: Precious metals or population? The English evidence", CEPR Discussion Paper 14023.

Eltis, D. and Engerman, S. (2000), "The importance of slavery and the slave trade to industrialising Britain", *Journal of Economic History*, Vol. 60, pp. 123–144.

Fischer, D. H. (1996), *The Great Wave and the Rhythm of History*, Oxford: Oxford University Press.

Frank, A. G. (1998), *Reorient: Global Economy in the Asian Age*, Berkeley: University of California Press.

Frankopan, P. (2015), *The Silk Roads: A New History of the World*, London: Bloomsbury.

Goldstone, J. A. (1991), "The causes of long waves in early modern economic history", *Research in Economic History*, Supp. 6, pp. 51–92.

Hamilton, E. (1934), *American Treasure and the Price Revolution in Spain*, Cambridge, MA: Harvard University Press.

Harris, J. R. (1988), *The British Iron Industry*, Basingstoke: Macmillan.

Inikori, J. E. (2002), *Africans and the Industrial Revolution in England: A Study in International Trade and Economic Development*, Cambridge: Cambridge University Press.

Kamen, H. (2003), *Empire: How Spain Became a World Power, 1492–1763*, New York: Harper Collins.

Kamen, H. (2014), *Spain 1469–1714: A Society of Conflicts*, London and New York: Longman.

Kenwood, A. G. and Lougheed, A. L. (1983), *The Growth of the International Economy, 1820–1960*, London: Routledge.

Keynes, J. M. (1930), *A Treatise on Money*, New York: Harcourt Brace Company.

McCusker, J. and Menard, R. (1991), *The Economy of British America: 1607–1789*, Chapel Hill: University of North Carolina Press.

Minchinton, W. E. (1969), *The Growth of English Overseas Trade in the Seventeenth and Eighteenth Centuries*, London: Routledge.

Motavasseli, A. and Smulders, S. (2017), "Urban and rural labour supply and home production, 1750–1830", Working Paper, Tilburg University.

Parthasarathi, P. (2011), *Why Europe Grew Rich and Asia Did Not: Global Economic Divergence, 1600–1850*, Cambridge: Cambridge University Press.

Richardson, D. (1998), "The British Empire and the Atlantic slave trade, 1660–1807" in Marshall, P. J. (ed.), *The Oxford History of the British Empire*, Vol. 3, Oxford: Oxford University Press.

Richardson, D. (2003), "Slave trade" in Mokyr, J. (ed.), *The Oxford Encyclopaedia of Economic History*, Oxford: Oxford University Press.

Williams, E. (1944), *Capitalism and Slavery*, Richmond: University of North Carolina Press.

5 Conclusion

The conclusion can be brief. In this monograph we have emphasised the importance of the British control of India for the emergence of modern economic growth. While we accept that the discovery of huge deposits of silver in Mexico and Peru in the sixteenth century and the Atlantic slave trade both had important consequences for global trade and global development (including slave labour being the rock on which a modern economy was built in the USA),[1] we remain, for reasons discussed, less than convinced that they could have been or were the predominant factors behind the emergence of modern economic growth. Instead, it seems to us that the far more important factors were the British victory at Plassey (1757),[2] which gave the British EIC the political control over Bengal (the richest province in India at that time), and subsequently the gaining of the *Diwani* – the responsibility of civil administration – of Bengal and access to its revenue following the victory in the Battle of Buxar (1764). Britain would then go on to colonise the rest of India from this base.

There was constant warfare in India at that time while the Mughal Empire was disintegrating. Many groups were competing for power. How did then a company of foreign merchants triumph over powerful and militaristic Indian Kings? A number of explanations have been offered, but the most important reason would appear to be that the Company had better access to resources to fight and win wars. EIC could not only draw on its own financial system to fund its military ventures, it also, as we have just noted, had seized control of the wealthy Gangetic plains. The revenue generation potentials of the Gangetic plains were much higher than elsewhere in India. The EIC was also able to levy higher taxes (it has been claimed via offering

DOI: 10.4324/9781003715368-5

elite a land market in return for higher levies (see Roy 2013)). Bengal revenue more than doubled within 25 years of the Company rule. The increase was achieved not by making land produce more, but wholly by wresting more from the landlords (Roy 2013, p. 35). In contrast, other competing powers in India had high potential costs of raising revenues to fight and strife over rights to rule (Hoffman 2015).

The opium revenue would also appear to have played an important role in this context. The Company was by the 1790s beginning to get substantial revenue from the sale of opium to China. Opium revenue accounted for 8 per cent of the British Indian land revenue in the early years and then rose to as high as 16 per cent. The debt service as a percentage of revenue was considerably lower for the EIC than for the competing powers. In British India, in the decade of the Third Anglo-Maratha War (1817–1818), debt service as a percentage of revenue fell from nearer 20 per cent to 12 per cent (see Sykes 1859; see also Roy 2013). This was the time when opium revenue was beginning to become highly significant. As a Chinese historian put it, from the opium trade, China got the opium, British the silver and India the (British) Raj (see Wong 1998). Without the opium revenue, the expansion of British rule in India would have been greatly constrained.

Be that as it may, there is no doubt that the increasing sums of money allowed the Company to build up the strength of its army. The Company's inability to attract sufficient numbers of Europeans to its forces forced the Company to seek recruits from the large mercenary labour market then existing in India. The Company was in a buyer's market.

Indians seemed to have had a number of reasons for joining the Company's army. There are strong indications, however, that the prime attraction of the Company's service was that it paid more regularly than the Indian princes.[3] And in due course, the Royal Navy and the Indian Army would go on to become "the hammer and anvil" of the British power in the world.

It is India which made Britain the pre-eminent economic and military power. It is British policies and actions, based on her Indian foundation, that led to the globalisation of the nineteenth century – a globalisation very different from the previous globalisations in history. Technological innovations of the nineteenth century were embedded in that globalisation process. It is this which ensured that growth and innovations would not peter out this time as they had after various "efflorescences" in history. If one is looking for a decisive disjuncture that opened the path to modern economic growth, then that disjuncture, we submit, is to be found in the British victory at Plassey.

Notes

1 See the discussion in Chapter 2.
2 In 1756 the British East India Company had provoked an attack from Siraj-ud-daulah, the young Nawab of Bengal. With the help of the conspirators from Nawab's camp and deserters from the Nawab's army at the last moment, Clive defeated the Nawab in the Battle of Plassey in the following year.
3 cf. Bryant (2000).

References

Bryant, G. J. (2000), "Indigenous mercenaries in the service of European imperialists: The case of the Sepoys in the early British Indian Army, 1750–1800", *War in History,* Vol. 7, pp. 2–28.

Hoffman, P. (2015), *Why Did Europe Conquer the World?*, Princeton: Princeton University Press.

Roy, T. (2013), "Rethinking the origins of British India: State formation and military-fiscal undertakings in an eighteenth century world region", *Modern Asian Studies*, Vol. 47, pp. 1125–1156.

Sykes, W. H. (1859), "The past, present, and prospective financial conditions of British India", *Journal of the Statistical Society of London*, Vol. 22, pp. 455–480.

Wong, J. Y. (1998), *Deadly Dreams: Opium, Imperialism, and the Arrow War (1856–1860) in China, Cambridge Studies in Chinese History, Literature and Institutions*, Cambridge: Cambridge University Press.

Index